"[…] being a Raised Master in the Masonic Fraternity as well as a Master Magician in *Ordo Templi Orientis* (O.T.O.), one of the few remaining Orders instructing its members in practical magick, Jaime Paul Lamb has one foot firmly planted in both these camps, Masonic and Magical. He thus speaks with authority on the hidden connections between Freemasonry and Ceremonial Magick. Moreover, he does a fine job of demonstrating those occult connections to his readers."

—P.D. Newman, 32°, author of *Alchemically Stoned*

"Jaime Paul Lamb's new book provides a good starting point for the study of Freemasonry's esoteric roots, from the overlap between Masonry and ceremonial magick that flourished in the early part of the twentieth century, to solar and astronomical symbolism in the Fraternity, and finally to elements of classical mythology that can be found to this day among Masonic teachings. All of these subjects offer vast fields for further inquiry, and this book will give you a solid foundation from which to explore them."

—Scott Michael Stenwick, author of
Arcana and *Mastering the Mystical Heptarchy*

"Jaime Paul Lamb has captured the essence of the subtle elements of Freemasonry and has condensed them into a highly readable and informative book. This is a welcomed addition to the body of knowledge of the Craft."

— William S. Burkle, Ph.D.,
MM, KT, 32°, SRICF IX°

"Jaime Paul Lamb is a tremendous talent. He offers an exciting opportunity for the Speculative Freemason to enrich his understanding of the craft."

— David Miller, 33°, KCT, IX°
and Chief Adept of SRICF Arizona College

MYTH, MAGICK & MASONRY

OCCULT PERSPECTIVES IN FREEMASONRY

JAIME PAUL LAMB
KT, 32°, SRICF VII°, OTO III°

THE LAUDABLE PURSUIT PRESS

Published by The Laudable Pursuit Press.
2018

Edited by Jason E. Marshall, 32º

Book design and layout by Matthew D. Anthony, 32º

ISBN: 978-1-7326214-0-4

The Laudable Pursuit
www.thelaudablepursuit.com
Email: editor@thelaudablepursuit.com

Printed by Lulu.com

ACKNOWLEDGEMENTS

I would like to offer my sincerest gratitude to my wife, Stephanie, for her patience and to the members of the following fraternal orders and societies, of which I am a current or past member, for their invaluable guidance and support:

Old Well-St John's Lodge no. 6, F. & A.M., Norwalk, CT
South Pasadena Lodge no. 290, F. & A.M., South Pasadena, CA
Arizona Lodge no. 2, F. & A.M., Phoenix, AZ
Ascension Lodge U.D., F. & A.M., Phoenix, AZ
A.A.S.R. of Freemasonry, N.M.J., Valley of Bridgeport, CT
A.A.S.R. of Freemasonry, S.J., Valley of Pasadena, CA
Arizona Chapter no. 1, Royal Arch Masons, York Rite, Phoenix, AZ
Phoenix Council no. 4, Cryptic Masons, York Rite, Phoenix, AZ
Phoenix Commandery no. 3, Knights Templar, York Rite, Phoenix, AZ
Arizona Research Lodge no. 1, Phoenix, AZ
Societas Rosicruciana in Civitatibus Foederatis, Arizona College
The Scottish Rite Research Society
Tahuti Lodge, *Ordo Templi Orientis*, New York City, NY
Star Sapphire Lodge, *Ordo Templi Orientis*, Los Angeles, CA
Lapis Lazuli Oasis, *Ordo Templi Orientis*, Phoenix, AZ
B.O.T.A. Hermetic Qabalah Study Group, Los Angeles, CA
B.O.T.A. Hermetic Qabalah Study Group, Phoenix, AZ

I am also indebted, of course, to the work of my predecessors and contemporaries in Masonic and occult research. Please peruse the titles in the bibliography appended to this volume for a somewhat comprehensive list of the works that I have personally found to be indispensable to my studies.

I would like to thank P.D. Newman, 32°, a man and Mason whose work I greatly admire, for contributing the foreword to this volume and for his invaluable guidance throughout the project; my friend and brother Ernest Williams, M.A. for his helpful insight in the initial editing process; my fellow fratres in Masonic Rosicrucianism, John A. Nichols, PM, 32°, KCCH, KT, SRICF VIII° and Briggs B. Cunningham, and also Reverend Albert Peter Krueger for proofreading. Many thanks to Richard Kaczynski for the crucial, last-minute suggestions for review.

Lastly, I would like to thank Jason Marshall and Matt Anthony of The Laudable Pursuit for editing, formatting, executing the art and layout, and for publishing my manuscript, in particular, and also for their work in promoting the advancement of Masonic thought and letters, in general. This book is dedicated to those seeking further Light in Freemasonry or upon any other path in the Western Esoteric Tradition. It is my hope that you find something of value in my labors.

Sincerely & Fraternally,
Jaime Paul Lamb
Phoenix, AZ
A.L.6017

TABLE OF CONTENTS

FOREWORD ....*xi*

INTRODUCTION by P.D. Newman, 32° ....*xv*

SECTION I:
The Integral Relationship Between Freemasonry and Ceremonial Magick.. *1*

SECTION II:
Solar and Astrological Symbolism in Freemasonry *39*

SECTION III:
Elements of Classical Mythology in Modern Freemasonry *75*

SECTION IV:
Freemasonry and the Rites of Mithras

BIBLIOGRAPHY *121*

INDEX *127*

FOREWORD

As I discussed in my paper *KING SOLOMON: Master Mason, Master Magician*, Masonic legend relates that Solomon's temple was built by "three Grand Masters, three thousand and three hundred Masters, or Overseers of the Work, eighty thousand Fellow-Crafts, and seventy thousand Entered Apprentices or bearers of the burthens [sic]."[1] However, the magical tradition of Islam tells a very different story.

According to Moslem religious historian Sheikh al-Siuti, in constructing his magnificent temple Solomon "assembled all the wisest men [and] genii...of the earth, and the mightiest of the devils, and appointed one division of them to build, another to cut blocks and columns from the marble mines, and others to dive into ocean-depths, and fetch therefrom pearls and coral. ...So he began to build the Temple. [The] devils cut quarries of jacinth and emerald. Also the devils made highly-polished cemented blocks of marble."[2]

In the Islamic tradition, our esteemed Masonic Grand Master King Solomon is not only a wise and powerful Hebrew king, he is also, as Thelemic Freemason Lon Milo DuQuette described him in his book *The Key to Solomon's Key*, "an audacious oriental wizard [who] could talk with animals, fly through the air on a magic carpet, and cause others to fly through the air to him. He could control the powers of nature and was master of the denizens of the spirit world, the demons...and genii of Shahrazad's *A Thousand and One Arabian Nights*." Solomon is, therefore, also a *Master Magician*.

Solomon mastered and controlled these demons, devils, and genii with the assistance of a series magical incantations and seals. Utilizing the same, he held the "denizens of the spirit world" captive in mysterious brazen vessels, not unlike the lamp possessed by the peasant boy in the *Aladdin* tale.

The means by which the wise King Solomon would summon these spirits, along with their names, ranks, seals, and powers, were inscribed and preserved in a number of 15th and 16th century magical texts known as *Solomonic grimoires*. These detail many of the spirits of which Solomon is said to have made use, possibly even in the building of his temple. Solomon may therefore be viewed as the *corpus callosum* bridging Freemasonry and Ceremonial Magick, the left and right hemispheres of the same esoteric *brain*.

---

1   *The New Masonic Trestleboard*, Moore, CW Moore Publishing, 1868.
2   DuQuette, *The Key to Solomon's Key*, CCC Publishing, 2010.

Not unlike King Solomon, being a Raised Master in the Masonic Fraternity as well as a Master Magician in the *Ordo Templi Orientis* (O.T.O.), one of the few remaining Orders instructing its members in practical magick, Jaime Paul Lamb has one foot firmly planted in both these camps, Masonic and Magical. He thus speaks with authority on the hidden connections between Freemasonry and Ceremonial Magick. Moreover, he does a fine job of demonstrating those occult connections to his readers.

P.D. Newman, 32°
Author of *Alchemically Stoned*

INTRODUCTION

My decision to petition for membership in the Masonic Fraternity was based on some research and investigation into the Western Esoteric Tradition that I had done during a transitional time in my life. I was in the process of trying to affect some fundamental lifestyle changes – part of a larger process of refinement that had long been underway – when I had the good fortune of coming across a copy of Manly P. Hall's *Secret Teachings of All Ages*, which was recommended to me by a friend. This exposure could not have happened at a more opportune time. It seemed as though the door to a hidden world with its own shadowy personages, noumena/phenomena and bizarre history had suddenly opened. I was irresistibly attracted to this arcane landscape as if there were a great Mystery to be unraveled – and indeed there was.

With all of the attendant cross-referencing, online research and supplementary reading that a thoughtful and thorough pursuit of the endeavor required, it took me slightly over a year to finish the book. Before I was a third of the way through, however, I had petitioned my local Masonic Lodge (Old Well-St Johns Lodge no. 6, A. & F.M., chartered in 1765 at Norwalk, CT). The decision to join the Fraternity had become obvious to me, as becoming a Freemason was a necessary step on my projected path going forward.

Upon my first few visits to the Lodge, I initially feared that the Fraternity had devolved into a sort of diner's club or social order, devoid of any connection to the occult lineage of the Mysteries I had read about. I was reassured, however, on the night of my Entered Apprentice initiation, when I began to get an inkling of the Craft's true esoteric import. Throughout that initiation (and the initiations, lectures and catechisms that followed, both in the Blue Lodge and the appendant bodies and societies to which I had later gained entry), I was exposed to what Hall had called "Freemasonry's priceless heritage". Though this information lay behind a veneer of relatively obvious moral and ethical lessons, I came to realize, in time, that the Fraternity had become the custodian of a body of ritual and symbolism whose origins were of inestimable antiquity and of considerable occult value – but the development of a sufficient set of interpretive tools, with which to unlock and decipher the Hidden Mysteries of Freemasonry, was first necessary.

The present work is comprised of four individually discrete Sections – each utilizing an alternate interpretive lens through which one may examine the ritualism and symbolism of Freemasonry – that reflect a culmination of some of the work that I had done to develop a few distinct reference points. The essays comprising this book were written between August of 2012 and July of 2017 for presentations in St. Johns Lodge no. 6, F. & A.M. Norwalk, CT, South Pasadena Lodge no. 290, F. & A.M. South Pasadena, CA, the Arizona College of the *Societas Rosicruciana in Civitabus Foederatis* and Arizona Research Lodge no. 1 (for which body I served as Worshipful Master for the year 2016). Excerpts from Sections II, III and IV have been edited into short articles and previously published in the *Connecticut Freemason* and *Indiana Freemason* magazines, and on The Laudable Pursuit website (www.thelaudablepursuit.com).

These essays were initially written for a Masonic audience and, in that, may pose some problems for a non-Masonic readership. I have, however, done my best to universalize some of the concepts and thereby render them more accessible to the non-Mason. Those non-Masons who have participated in other initiatory orders within the greater Western Mystery Tradition should be able to find value in this information, analogous to their specific initiatory lineage. In the end, my line of reasoning was that: if one is interested in the content of this book, then one will likely bring at least a cursory understanding of the subject matter coming into the endeavor. That being said, this book is not the best place to start if one is entirely unfamiliar with the general concepts, history and narratives of either Ceremonial Magick, Mithraism, Classical Mythology, astrological/ solar/stellar lore, or Freemasonry. Many of the titles in the bibliography at the back of this volume may be of supplementary value. I have also cited my sources – this should be helpful in fleshing out some of the ideas in the text and, of course, in corroborating the referenced information.

Lastly, I would like to say a few words to the brethren of all Regular, UGLE-recognized Masonic Lodges (F. & A.M. and A.F. & A.M) and in Freemasonry's several appendant bodies. Reference has been made, in these essays, to our Modes of Recognition and also to subject matter which would certainly fall under the banner of Masonic secrets. Like all Regular Masons, I have been obligated to "always hele, forever conceal and never reveal" these secrets; and I am confident that they are secure herein. Though some of the signs, words and grips, et cetera, are either alluded to or explicitly mentioned in passing, they are never specifically mentioned as being such; to *profani*, such references are merely included to provide context and elucidation. Let us not forget that these words were in use before their adoption in Masonic ritual (with the possible exception of the substitute for the Master's Word, which is, of course, not given herein), and that these words are still currently used in theological, mythological and literary contexts, thus one would not suspect their Masonic import. Therefore, only those to whom the Modes of Recognition have been lawfully entrusted will be able to discern the Masonically sensitive material with any certainty. This being the case, there are several passages throughout the present work which will likely be glanced over without a second thought by the uninitiated – though these same passages may contain information quite significant to the Freemason.

In the end, with all the secrets of the Craft visible to anyone with access to *Duncan's Ritual* (or, of course, an internet search engine), my reasoning is that the symbolism, rituals and degree work in Freemasonry are strictly experiential and no amount of superficial knowledge of them could ever take the place of an authentic and empirical, first-hand apprehension of our Mysteries. One could, for instance, write a ten thousand-page tome, graphically and minutely describing the experience of, say, eating an orange – the weight of it in the hand, the scent of the mist spritzing from the rind when peeled, the sweetness, the acidity, et cetera – yet they could never duplicate or replace the experience itself. There is simply no substitute for a human beings' sensory organs working in concert with his or her imagination to create a picture of the world; its objects, phenomena and events. Such is the experiential nature of the initiatory path of the Mysteries – *things done, things heard and things seen*, as it were.

It is my hope that my brother Masons, whether those who have been newly raised or those who have been with us for a while, find enough inspirational and thought-provoking material in the present volume to reevaluate and perhaps deepen their connection with the Craft of Freemasonry and the lessons inculcated within it.

SECTION I:

THE INTEGRAL RELATIONSHIP BETWEEN FREEMASONRY AND CEREMONIAL MAGICK

THE INTEGRAL RELATIONSHIP BETWEEN FREEMASONRY AND CEREMONIAL MAGICK

"The Occult Science of the Ancient Magi was concealed under the shadows of the Ancient Mysteries: it was imperfectly revealed or rather disfigured by the Gnostics: it is guessed at under the obscurities that cover the pretended crimes of the Templars; and it is found enveloped in enigmas that seem impenetrable, in the Rites of the Highest Masonry."[1]

Freemasonry and Ceremonial Magick are generally considered to be mutually exclusive systems with their only conspicuous connection being that both traditions may periodically be encountered in the vicinity of hermeticism. However, it can be demonstrated that the long-running process of cross-fertilization which has occurred between these two seemingly disparate traditions has left both irreversibly altered; and further, that to extract the qualities of one from the other would render one system formally unrecognizable and the other substantially anemic. Ceremonial Magick would be stripped of its formal structure leaving but a loosely related and amorphous jumble of primitive and arcane rites, devoid of a greater systematic context. While Freemasonry's towering structures would be reduced to mere scaffolding – a gentlemen's society bereft of theurgical intercession, mystic and transformative rites of initiation, and the Fraternity's evocative ritual-dramas, all steeped in the Ancient Mystery Traditions.

The recognizable structure of modern Ceremonial Magick (most popularly represented by the Hermetic Order of the Golden Dawn system and its offshoots) is largely based on Masonic ritual. Conversely, the mystical or numinous quality of Masonic ritual represents the vestigial remnants of the Mystery Traditions of the Western World, which served as the ancient storehouses of collected wisdom and magick. The magical and alchemical systems collected under the banner of hermeticism share common thematic elements with Freemasonry, perhaps best exemplified by their observance of the sympathetic relationship between the microcosm and the

---

1   Pike, Morals and Dogma, L. H. Jenkins Inc., 1947, p. 83.

macrocosm.[2] This dynamic is referred to in more recent 'New Thought' literature as the Hermetic Principle of Correspondence[3], which is a modern distillation of this ancient hermetic concept. Roman Mithraism also represents a coherent link between the Magian tradition of the Persian *magi* and modern Craft Freemasonry, thus illustrating a direct magical current in the latter.[4] Taking all the evidence into account, we will find that Freemasonry and Ceremonial Magick are not merely complimentary, but that their synergetic relationship is an integral and, ultimately, indispensable component of each system.

Before moving on, it is first necessary that we briefly establish a definition of our terms in order to formulate a coherent historical and conceptual orientation; and for those readers who may be unfamiliar with our subjects. This is universally admitted to be a formidable task, since the origins of each tradition disappear into the mists of prehistory; however, we shall endeavor to define our terms specifically as they relate to the subject at hand.

OPERATIVE AND SPECULATIVE FREEMASONRY

The operative roots of Freemasonry can be traced as far back as the construction of the prehistoric world's megalithic structures, which were erected not long after the last glacial thaw, at the dawn of the Neolithic Era.[5] These first architectural methods were devised for the express purpose of being executed in worked stone.[6] Over the course of the next several millennia, these once simple structures evolved in complexity as knowledge of mathematics in general, and geometry in particular, increased. From the beginning, we see an adherence to astronomical formations and considerations as to the orientation of said structures.[7] As the operative craft of Masonry progressed over time and migrated across the ancient world, so too did the body of the operative Mason's 'best developed practices'. By the end of the first millennium CE, these included various sets of by-laws, constitutions and rules of conduct pertaining to the governance of the largely autonomous Mason's guilds, and the cor-

---

2   Quispel, *The Way of Hermes: New Translations of The Corpus Hermeticum and the Definitions of Hermes Trismegistus to Asclepius*, Inner Traditions, 2004, Preface.
3   Three Initiates, *The Kybalion*, Yogi Publication Society Masonic Temple, 1912, p. 5.
4   Vail, *The Ancient Mysteries and Modern Masonry*, Forgotten Books, 2012, p. 45-50.
5   Scham, *The World's First Temple*, Archaeology Magazine, Dec. 2008, p. 23.
6   Ibid. p. 23.
7   Lockyer, *Stonehenge and Other British Stone Monuments Astronomically Considered*, sacred-texts.com, 1909, p. 62.

pus of trade secrets. The communication of this information was limited to the class of the ancient builder and was likely transmitted hereditarily. It would logically follow that these secrets were then meted out by a sequential degree system, relative to the workman's stage of development within the operative craft, as evidenced by the natural sociological tendency to hierarchical stratification, common to all trades since time immemorial.[8] Additionally, this degree system – and the accompanying signs, words and tokens associated with each established skill level – would serve as the professional hallmark of the traveling workman. The distribution of the operative Mason's wages was also contingent upon the craftsman being able to communicate his status within the guild. The degrees of proficiency within the medieval craft guilds, as in many trades today, were (from bottom to top): *Apprentice* (known in speculative Masonry as *Entered Apprentice*), *Journeyman* (known as *Fellowcraft*) and *Master Mason*.

Many, if not all masons of the Middle Ages learnt their craft through an informal apprentice system. They would generally be members of a guild comprised of different artistic styles and varying skill levels. There were three main classes of stonemasons. They were the apprentice, journeymen and the master mason. At a cathedral construction site, the master mason is usually the head and he oversees the work of all skilled and unskilled laborers. His army of workmen will include carpenters, layers, metal-smiths, carriers, rope makers, and even occasionally animals—oxen. What the medieval mason lacked in technology, he made up for it in ingenuity and personal skill. The combination and coordination of their collective skills are what gave us the architectural miracle we see today.[9]

Speculative Freemasonry, popularly defined as "a science of morality, veiled in allegory and illustrated by symbols"[10] consists of a system of three sequential, initiatory rites known as *degrees*, designed to inculcate moral and ethical lessons in the mind of the initiate, primarily through the use of lectures, catechisms and the portrayal of ritual-drama. The Craft draws much of its symbolic and allegorical content from operative stonemasonry

8   Mackey, *The Symbolism of Freemasonry*, Forgotten Books, 2012, pp. 47-48.
9   Akande, *Medieval Masons and Gothic Cathedrals*, 2016. Society of Architectural Historians, www.sah.org, retrieved online.
10   Mackey, *The Symbolism of Freemasonry*, Forgotten Books, 2012, p. 10.

as well as elements of the Old Testament narrative of the building of King Solomon's Temple.

Operative stonemason guilds became more and more populated by speculative, or accepted, Masons throughout the 17th and 18th centuries. These accepted Masons, who did not practice the physical craft of stonemasonry, adopted the vernacular and degree system of the operative Masons, whose offices, implements and nomenclature had already been in the long process of being imbued with symbolic import. For instance, manual stonemason's tools such as the plumb, level and square were given a correspondingly moral interpretation based upon the attributes of the instrument. The elements and paraphernalia of operative stonemasonry were ritualistically employed in allegorized lessons, set in and around the building of King Solomon's Temple, wherein the biblical personas associated with the narrative – King Solomon, Hiram King of Tyre and Hiram Abiff – are portrayed.

> *Now, the operative art having, for us, ceased, we, as speculative Masons, symbolize the labors of our predecessors by engaging in the construction of a spiritual temple in our hearts, pure and spotless, fit for the dwelling-place of Him who is the author of purity--where God is to be worshipped in spirit and in truth, and whence every evil thought and unruly passion is to be banished, as the sinner and the Gentile were excluded from the sanctuary of the Jewish temple. This spiritualizing of the temple of Solomon is the first, the most prominent and most pervading of all the symbolic instructions of Freemasonry. It is the link that binds the operative and speculative divisions of the order. It is this which gives it its religious character. Take from Freemasonry its dependence on the temple, leave out of its ritual all reference to that sacred edifice, and to the legends connected with it, and the system itself must at once decay and die, or at best remain only as some fossilized bone, imperfectly to show the nature of the living body to which it once belonged.[11]*

---

11   Mackey, *The Symbolism of Freemasonry*, Forgotten Books, 2012.

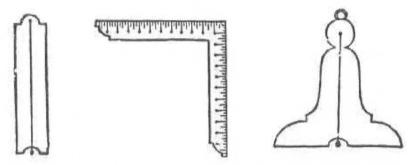

The Plumb, Level and Square – the symbolic working tools of Speculative Freemasonry and the jewels associated with the Junior Warden, Worshipful Master and Senior Warden, respectively.

MAGICK

By the term magick (note the archaic Early Modern English spelling, terminating with a K, which "has been adopted throughout in order to distinguish the Science of the Magi from all its counterfeits"[12], and also differentiates this form of magic from that of the stage), we recognize the Crowleyan definition: "the Science and Art of causing Change in conformity with Will".[13] This definition, or slight variations upon it, stands as the popular working definition in most modern magical communities from the early 20th century to the present and is sufficiently concise for our purposes.

While it is true that the modern conception of Ceremonial Magick (also referred to as "High Magic") is inextricably linked to certain developments in 19th century occultism, there remains a clear and traceable path of influence leading backward into antiquity to the remotest periods of primitive ritual construction. The origin of Ceremonial Magick is essentially indistinguishable from that of Natural Magic; with minor differing elements such as the compositional complexity of the rituals, the structural complexity of the consecrated paraphernalia employed and the practice of theurgical intervention. Since no discernible demarcation of simplicity vs. complexity exists, the practical differences between these two magical paradigms are largely nominal. In the final analysis, when considering the tributary origins of Ceremonial Magick, we are free to avail ourselves to

---

12   Crowley, *Liber ABA, Book 4, Part II*, Weiser, 2008, p. 47.
13   Ibid., p. 126.

the lineal influence of Natural Magic.

In its currently practiced form, Ceremonial Magick is primarily distinguished by its long and elaborate operations, the many accessories that aid in the execution of its rituals, and the intercession of angels, daemons, djinn and other entities. This magical paradigm was popularized by several hermetic, qabalistic, Rosicrucian and quasi-Masonic magical societies operating during the 19th century and early part of the 20th century; a period of time which has come to be known as the Golden Age of Fraternalism.

> *The main principles are summed in the conception of a number of assumed mysterious forces in the universe which could be put in operation by man, or at least followed in their secret processes. In the ultimate, however, they could all be rendered secondary, if not passive, to the will of man; for even in astrology, which was the discernment of forces regarded as peculiarly fatal, there was an art of ruling, and sapiens dominabitur astris became an axiom of the science. This conception culminated or centred in the doctrine of unseen, intelligent powers, with whom it was possible for prepared persons to communicate; the methods by which this communication was attempted are the most important processes of Magic, and the books which embody these methods, called Ceremonial Magic, are the most important part of the literature.[14]*

While being the lineal ancestor of Ceremonial Magick, Natural Magic (sometimes referred to as "Low Magic") is differentiated by virtue of its operations dealing directly with natural forces as opposed to utilizing angelic or daemonic intervention. Natural Magic utilizes astrology, alchemy and other disciplines that have developed into the natural sciences of today; astrology has become astronomy, alchemy has become chemistry, et cetera, and, therefore, may be viewed as proto-scientific. Notably, Natural Magic has less of an inherent concentration of hermetic and qabalistic content than Ceremonial Magick.

> *Natural Magic is commonly used by followers of various Pagan paths, ranging from solitaries and Hedge Witches to members of traditional covens. In the past, Paganism was most frequently associated with people of the fields. Since they didn't*

---

14   Waite, *The Book of Ceremonial Magic*, 1913, www.sacred-texts.com, retrieved online.

have lots of irrigation systems, they needed to be in lower lands where water from rains would accumulate for their crops. As a result, Natural Magic is also known as "Low Magic." This should not imply that it is in any way lower, of less value, or less spiritual than other forms of magic, only that its European sources were in the fertile lowlands.[15]

At length, we may consider Ceremonial Magick a syncretized descendant of Natural Magic, the modern conception of which is intimately related to the formation of the Hermetic Order of the Golden Dawn and other 19th and 20th century magical orders. Significantly, the Golden Dawn was formed by three Freemasons – William Wynn Westcott, Samuel Liddell MacGregor Mathers and Dr. William Robert Woodman – all of whom were members of the invitational Masonic order, the Societas Rosicruciana in Anglia.[16]

It seems that, perhaps since the end of the 19th century occult revival, the Regular Blue Lodge Freemason has not been adequately instructed to perceive the often cryptic occult motifs present in Masonic ritual. This is likely because he has neither been mentored from the perspective of the hermetic arts, nor has he been given the impetus to independently develop the necessary reference points allowing him to distinguish the hallmarks of Ceremonial Magick, such as sephirothic configurations, gematriac numerical significance, invocational and evocational passages and other magical operations and formulas. This is a matter which we hope to begin to rectify in this Section of the present work.

Similarly, the modern Ceremonial Magick practitioner often fails to observe that the lion's share of their ritual and Grade system – such as that of the Golden Dawn and *Ordo Templi Orientis*, for example – is patterned on long-established Masonic ritualism and Rosicrucian-inherited fraternal structure; not to mention the fact that the very idea of Ceremonial Magick, by and large, comes to us in its modern form almost solely due to Masonic scholarship and restoration.[17]

---

15   Kraig, *Natural Magic (Low Magic)*, Llewelyn Encyclopedia, www.llewellyn.com, retrieved online.
16   Regardie, *The Golden Dawn*, Llewellyn, 2014, pp. 16-18.
17   Ibid. pp. 16-18.

Levi, *Transcendental Magic: Its Doctrine And Ritual,* Martino, 2011, p. 240

HERMETICISM'S CONTRIBUTION TO FREEMASONRY AND MAGICK

The correspondences between hermeticism and Freemasonry are best made evident by two factors: the archetypally hermetic and/or mercurial character of some of the Masonic Lodge officer's roles (which will be discussed in Section III of the present volume) and by an observance of the sympathetic relationship between the microcosm and macrocosm; particularly as this dynamic is described in the 1st through 4th century writings attributed to *Hermes Trismegistus*[18] and a 6th century document called the *Tabula Smaragdina,* also known as the *Emerald Tablet.*[19] One of the areas in

---

18   Salaman, Oyen, et al., *The Way of Hermes: New Translations of The Corpus Hermeticum and the Definitions of Hermes Trismegistus to Asclepius,* Inner Traditions, 2004.
19   Goodrick-Clarke, *The Western Esoteric Traditions: A Historical Introduction,* Oxford University Press, 2008, p. 34.

which this relationship is made most readily apparent is architecture. The architectural conception of ancient megalithic edifices rested on a working knowledge of geometry, as does architecture today. Geometry, in turn, was predicated on an understanding of astronomy, since geometry (literally, *Earth measurement*) could only be perceived and calculated vis-à-vis the Earth's relative position to the fixed stars and the triangulation of coordinates thereby.[20] It is important to note the juxtaposition of the terrestrial and celestial globes atop the Masonic Lodge's Brazen Pillars and that the Fellowcraft Mason's attention is directed to them and he is told that "they are the noblest instruments for improving the mind"; note also the 47th Proposition of Euclid as it pertains to navigation, astronomical calculations and "Squaring the Temple", a practice that may be traced at least as far back as the use of a 3:4:5 triangle as a means of describing a 90° angle. Even a cursory study of the orientation and relative position of many ancient structures can confirm the irrefutable fact that these edifices were erected in keeping with the hermetic axiom, "that which is above is like that which is below"[21] and its Christianization, "on Earth as it is in Heaven".[22] These astronomically-aligned megalithic structures were generally oriented to equinoctial or solstitial points and were, in some cases, microcosmic terrestrial arrangements of macrocosmic celestial configurations, hermetically mirrored upon the Earth. This dynamic, which has persisted at least from the time of the ancient source documents through to reinterpretations in present day quasi-hermetic texts, also informs the practice of Ceremonial Magick in that a magical operation is a microcosmic model that is meant to influence the macrocosm through a sympathetic magical resonance. Due primarily to this sympathetic functionality, magick is counted among other hermetic arts – such as astrology and alchemy – which also share a similar dynamic.

> *This Principle embodies the truth that there is always a Correspondence between the laws and phenomena of the various planes of Being and Life. The old Hermetic axiom ran in these words: 'As above, so below; as below, so above.' And the grasping of this Principle gives one the means of solving many a dark paradox, and hidden secret of Nature. There are planes beyond our knowing, but when we apply the Principle of*

---

20   Aveni, *In Search of Ancient Astronomies*, Doubleday, 1978, pp. 165-202.
21   *quod est superius est sicut quod est inferius* – Polydorus, *De Alchimia*, Nuremburg, 1541, retrieved online.
22   *The Holy Bible* KJV, Matthew 6:9-13.

Correspondence to them we are able to understand much that would otherwise be unknowable to us. This Principle is of universal application and manifestation, on the various planes of the material, mental, and spiritual universe--it is an Universal Law. The ancient Hermetists considered this Principle as one of the most important mental instruments by which man was able to pry aside the obstacles which hid from view the Unknown. Its use even tore aside the Veil of Isis to the extent that a glimpse of the face of the goddess might be caught. Just as a knowledge of the Principles of Geometry enables man to measure distant suns and their movements, while seated in his observatory, so a knowledge of the Principle of Correspondence enables Man to reason intelligently from the Known to the Unknown. Studying the monad, he understands the archangel.[23]

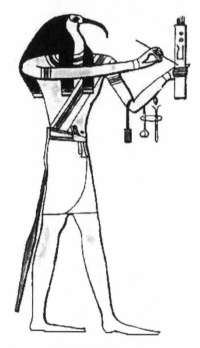

Thoth - Hermes

---

23   Three Initiates, *The Kybalion*, 1912, Yogi Publication Society Masonic Temple.

THE GENERAL BODY OF CORRESPONDENCES BETWEEN FREEMASONRY AND CEREMONIAL MAGICK

The parallels and synergetic relationships found between Freemasonry and Ceremonial Magick are many; to illuminate them all, particularly those of a subtler nature, would merely belabor the issue and possibly obscure the point. It is in this interest that we endeavor to examine a relatively small but pertinent body of correspondences, bearing in mind that these may be extrapolated to the minutest detail once an appropriately attuned perception has been developed.

In Ceremonial Magick, temple spaces are often oriented East-to-West – or, at the very least, to the symbolic East and West – as are all Masonic Lodge rooms. The orientation of the Masonic Lodge room is said to be based upon that of King Solomon's Temple although, interestingly, it faces the opposite direction. The door of King Solomon's Temple (and many other ancient temples) was in the East, thereby letting the rising sun illuminate the *Sanctum Sanctorum*, or Holy of Holies, particularly on the morning of the vernal equinox (which will be discussed in further detail in the Solar and Astrological Section of the present volume). Conversely, the door of the Masonic Lodge room is in the West. This may be the case because of another hermetic allusion regarding man's status vis-à-vis Deity. The lessons of Freemasonry explicitly detail a process by which a good man may become better by virtue of his own good works – the Rough Ashlar being transformed into the Perfect Ashlar by the application of the speculative Working Tools of Freemasonry, et cetera. Orienting the Masonic Lodge room (the House of Man) oppositely to the House of God (in this case, King Solomon's Temple), may very well constitute a cryptic Masonic commentary on the notion of salvation, not by God's grace alone, but by the individual's 'causing change in accordance with will' (note also that G.M.H.A. is interred in the West and is oriented as King Solomon's Temple was said to have been, thus further alluding to the macrocosmic Temple - a model of the Universe - being hermetically represented in the microcosmic man). Lodge rooms and magical Temples are also both noted to be microcosmic representations of the universe[24], again alluding to this hermetic sympathy.[25]

The two Brazen Pillars of the Blue Lodge, representing those on the

---

24   Mackey, *The Symbolism of Freemasonry*, Forgotten Books, 2012, p. 101.
25   Crowley, *Book 4, Part II*, Weiser, 2008, p. 49.

portico of King Solomon's Temple, are also present in most temples of Ceremonial Magick. As they architecturally pertain to astronomical orientation, these pillars have an immediate precedent in the obelisks of Dynastic Egypt (we will address this matter in greater detail in Section II). In the context of Ceremonial Magick, these pillars have been noted to be analogous to the qabalistic pillars of Severity and Mercy.[26] [27] In qabalism, these pillars are found flanking the Middle Pillar of the *Etz Chaim*, or Tree of Life.

> *These two pillars respectively connote also the active and passive expressions of Divine Energy, the Sun and the Moon, sulphur and salt, good and bad, light and darkness. Between them is the door leading into the House of God and standing thus at the gates of the Sanctuary they are a reminder that Jehovah is both an androgynous and an anthropomorphic Deity.*[28]

Fellowcraft degree tracing board, 1934

26   Regardie, *The Golden Dawn*, Llewellyn, 2014, p. 81.
27   Levi, *Transcendental Magic: Its Doctrine and Ritual*, Martino Publishing, 2011, pp. 37-44.
28   Hall, *The Secret Teachings of All Ages*, Dover, 2010 p. 262.

Some Masonic Lodges have a Chamber of Reflection adjoining the Lodge room in which the candidate is to contemplate their pending initiation. These chambers typically contain a desk and chair, pen and ink, a mirror, a candle, a skull, and will often display the acronym V.I.T.R.I.O.L. (*Visita Interiora Terrae Rectificando Invenies Occultum Lapidem*, which may be roughly translated as: 'visit the interior of the earth and [by] purifying [yourself] you will find the hidden stone'), or some other hermetic or alchemical maxim, written on the wall. The Chamber will oftentimes also contain a symbolic representation of the three philosophical principles: Salt, Sulfur and Mercury[29] (Salt, Sulfur and Mercury are the three primal alchemical properties of spagyric, or plant alchemy, which was popularized and likely coined by Paracelsus (Philippus Aureolus Theophrastus Bombastus von Hohenheim, Swiss, 1493-1541CE) in his book *Liber Paragranum*. The Alchemical Salt (Earth) is the refined basic salts, or alkaloids, extracted from the *Caput Mortuum*, or 'dead head', of the *Prima Materia*; the Alchemical Sulfur (Fire) is the distilled essential oil, and the Alchemical Mercury (Water) is the alcohol content yielded by the process of fermentation. In a basic spagyric alchemical operation, these three extractions are then recombined into the alchemically sublimated version of the *Prima Materia*, or First Matter, and the resultant tincture is then used as a holistic herbal remedy). This room fulfills the initiatory function of pre-liminal isolation common to many rites of passage[30] by providing an environment for the generation of a meditative consciousness and receptivity.

The Lodge room is banished (Banishment, in the present context, is magical parlance for the performance of a ritual, such as the Golden Dawn's Lesser Ritual of the Pentagram, which is intended to prepare and purify a magician's working space)[31] in several ways and at several times throughout the proceedings. First, the Junior Warden is instructed to inform the Tyler to keep off all "cowans and eavesdroppers" who, in this context, constitute the *profani*, or uninitiated. Second, at the opening of the ritual proper, the Grand Architect of the Universe – akin, here, to the occult concept of the egregore[32] – is evoked to "bless us in all our undertakings [...] bless our present assembling, and to enlighten our minds". At the ritual's closing, the Entity is asked to "pardon all that thy holy eye hath seen amiss in us while we have been together". The opening evocation is an invitation to the Entity to intervene in the theurgic work at hand. The closing entreaty

29   DaCosta, Jr., *The Chamber of Reflection*, freemasonry.bcy.ca, retrieved 2015.
30   Turner, *Forest of symbols: aspects of the Ndembu ritual*. Ithaca: Cornell UP, 1967, pp. 23–59.
31   Kraig, *Modern Magick*, Llewellyn, 1994, p. 525.
32   Delaforge, *The Templar Tradition: Yesterday and Today*, Gnosis Magazine no. 6, 1987.

constitutes a thankful dismissal of the Entity, common to many magical operations.[33] This dismissal effectively closes the theurgic communication and ceremonially demarcates the proceeding, thereby differentiating the ritualistic from the mundane. The evocations, banishment and dismissals of Ceremonial Magick are analogous to the opening and closing of a Masonic Lodge from abeyance to labor, and from labor to abeyance.

Myriad interpretive keys have been applied to the world's sacred texts. In addition to providing the standard moral and ethical rules of conduct for the particular culture of origin, the world's great body of theological and mythological literature has been shown to be comprised of allegorical material – symbolically depicting astronomical, agricultural and pro-creational cycles[34], in addition to magical, alchemical, entheogenic and archetypally psychological themes.[35] The use of the Volume of Sacred Law (often rendered as V.S.L. in Masonic literature, the usage of this term – as opposed to that of a specific Holy Book – is a testament to the universality of Freemasonry) in a Masonic ritual is in many respects analogous to the magician's use of a grimoire in that it may be used to provide the necessary personages, themes, narratives and paraphernalia for ritual construction and performance.

A grimoire is a compendium of rituals, operations and invocations, generally containing instructions on how to construct magical implements, potions and other paraphernalia. A 15th century grimoire entitled *The Book of Abramelin*, for example, contains the formula for an anointing oil called, fittingly, the Oil of Abramelin. This oil, which is used in the greater Abramelin operation, is actually very similar to a formula for anointing oil of the *Tanakh* found in the *Holy Bible*.

> *Then the* LORD *said to Moses, 'Take the following fine spices: 500 shekels of liquid myrrh, half as much (that is, 250 shekels) of fragrant cinnamon, 250 shekels of fragrant calamus, 500 shekels of cassia—all according to the sanctuary shekel— and a hin of olive oil. Make these into a sacred anointing oil, a fragrant blend, the work of a perfumer. It will be the sacred anointing oil'.*[36]

Freemason, Junior Substitute Magus of the *Societas Rosicrucia-*

---

33   Crowley, *Book 4, Part III*, Weiser, 2008, pp. 238-240.
34   Hall, *The Secret Teachings of All Ages*, Dover, 2010, pp. 94-98.
35   Jung, *Psychology and Alchemy*, Routledge and Kegan Paul, 1953, pp. 412-413.
36   *The Holy Bible*, KJV, Exodus 30:22-25.

na in Anglia, and Co-founder of the Hermetic Order of the Dawn, Samuel Liddell-MacGregor Mathers translated *The Book of Abramelin* from the original French and he made both the oil and the corresponding incense described in the volume [Though, likely due to the use of a faulty translation as his source document, it is generally believed that there was a substitution in his formula – Galangal for Calamus – which may or may not have been intentional]. Consequently, the Oil of Abramelin has become very popular in the Western Esoteric Tradition, particularly in Thelemic traditions such as *Ordo Templi Orientis* and the order's corresponding ecclesiastical body, *Ecclesia Gnostica Catholica.*

Magick words, formulas and acronyms such as LVX, I.N.R.I., V.I.T.R.I.O.L., ABRAC(H)ADABRA and the *Tetragrammaton* seem to have an intrinsic import on the level of the collective consciousness, due to these having been imbued with culturo-religious significance for centuries and, in some cases, millennia.[37] Masonic ritual contains many instances of words and passes used both as modes of recognition and as mnemonic keys, meant to bring an image or concept to mind such as "an ear of corn, hung near a water ford". In this sense, these words have been imbued with a similar sort of significance, in that they have become a microcosmic meme for the macrocosmic ritual, or magical operation, which they represent. At the mention of these words, which have been fused with experiential information, a flood of concepts, memories and empirical data comes gushing forth and the significance of the ritual or magical operation is once again recaptured. That certain words and formulas have become standards, common in magical and/or Masonic use, is analogous to a similar concept to that of the aforementioned egregore in that individual consciousnesses have coalesced into a sort of Platonic *ideal* or *form* of the given word or formula, held in the collective consciousness.

The Masonic Obligation, particularly as it pertains to proficiency and memorization, is a form of hypnotic auto-suggestion and, in this sense, is identical in function to a magical oath or pact.[38] The initiate, having been rendered psychically impressionable by the culmination of the preceding consciousness-altering aspects of the initiatory rite, is given a set of suggestions whose ultimate absorption and practice is designed to result in no less than moral and ethical behavior modification ('making good men better' et cetera). Magically, this constitutes a form of incantational enchantment – the Worshipful Master leads the initiate through a self-hypnotic and oath-bound spell, which calibrates the initiate's consciousness to an unflagging ad-

---

37   Crowley, *Book 4, Part III,* Weiser, 2008, pp. 168-173.
38   Ibid. p. 72.

herence to a new paradigm of self-development through *paternal* suggestion.

> *It is clear from Jung's writings that the way he was using hyp-*
> *nosis was what is called today 'paternal' hypnosis, i.e., the hyp-*
> *notist gives specific suggestions for attitude or behavior change*
> *to the entranced client. He referred to it as 'hypnotic suggestion*
> *therapy.'*[39]

As part of the Landmarks of the Fraternity, Masonic Obligations are predicated on the belief in a Supreme Being, for there would be no oath-binding authority in the absence of this clause. If we make note of the fact that the word *Being* is also defined as "the most important or basic part of a person's mind or self,"[40] it would follow that the achievement of the *Supreme* aspect of this state would be akin to the attainment of the in-dividuated or differentiated Self [41] – a Jungian concept, regarding a state of being in which all of the aspects of the psyche are brought into a coherent and integrated whole. The magical correlative of this state is often referred to as Knowledge and Conversation of one's Holy Guardian Angel and, in qabalistic terms, is associated with passing through the Veil of *Paroketh* into the *Sephirah* of *Tiphareth*.[42]

> *Behind Tiphareth, traversing the Tree, is drawn Paroketh,*
> *the Veil of the Temple, the analogue, on a lower plane, of the*
> *Abyss which separates the Three Supernals from the rest of the*
> *Tree. Like the Abyss, the Veil marks a chasm in consciousness.*
> *The mode of mentation on one side of the chasm differs in*
> *kind from the mode of mentation prevailing upon the other.*
> *Tiphareth is the highest sphere to which normal human con-*
> *sciousness can rise. When Philip said to Our Lord, "Show us*
> *the Father," Jesus replied, "He that hath seen Me hath seen the*
> *Father." All the human mind can know of Kether is its reflec-*
> *tion in Tiphareth, the Christ-centre, the Sphere of the Son.*
> *Paroketh is the Veil of the Temple which was rent asunder at*
> *the Crucifixion.*[43]

---

39   *Jung and Hypnotherapy*, Hartman and Zimberoff, Journal of Heart-Centered Therapies, 2013, Vol. 16, No. 1, p. 3.
40   www.merriam-webster.com, retrieved 2015.
41   Jung, *Collected Works*, Vol. 13, Bollingen, 1968, p. 67.
42   Fortune, *The Mystical Qabalah*, Weiser, 1998, p. 182.
43   Ibid., p. 45

Mandalas are symbols used in some traditions of Hinduism and Buddhism that are meant to be microcosmic representations of the universe – much like the Masonic Lodge room and the magician's temple – and are primarily utilized in generating contemplative and meditative consciousness. Similarly, Freemasonry's tracing boards are pictorial representations upon which the Mason may focus his attention in an effort to develop an interpretation of the material at a deeper level of consciousness than can be accomplished in another medium.[44]

The same may be said of other common symbols within the diagrammatic corpus of the Craft and, if we allow ourselves to venture slightly beyond the pale of the American Blue Lodge, we find the Mark Master Degree and its significance in terms of sigil magick. The Brother of this degree is charged to conceive of a simple and reduced, but subjectively meaningful mark, as a graphic means to differentiate his Work. This practice is in imitation of the ancient operative stonemasons whose wages were calculated by the appearance of their mark. The same practice is applied in sigil magick: the magician creates a simple, unique device as a representation of the projected fruition of the given magical operation. This is akin, in some respects, to the modern conception of a vision board, in that the sigil of the magician represents a concentration of his or her willed outcome. sigils are generally created by generating various correspondences that reflect the outcome of the magical operation and combining their reduced elements into one device.

The Point Within A Circle diagram, which will be discussed in further detail below, is an example of an established sigil within Freemasonry; however, its deepest import as a symbol is lost to conjecture.[45] Alternately, it could be argued that, the meaning and penetrative power of this sigil is subjective by design, never having been imbued with a particular interpretation, or otherwise defined. Myriad theories abound in the literature of Freemasonry regarding this device, ranging from the relatively mundane moral and ethical perspectives to that of practical geometry, through archaeo-astronomy and spiraling outward to the most convoluted metaphysical interpretations.[46]

Sigils, marks and devices such as these, like nearly every other component of Masonry's symbolic and allegorical content, serve as a means to bypass the hyper-differentiated, egoic mind and infiltrate the unconscious – perhaps even stimulating an exchange with the collective unconscious,

---

44   Jung, *Man and His Symbols*, Doubleday, 1964, p. 55.
45   Mackey, *The Symbolism of Freemasonry*, Forgotten Books, 2012, pp. 111-116.
46   Ibid. pp. 111-116.

as proposed by C.G. Jung.[47] The means by which we absorb the ritual and symbolism of Freemasonry are part and parcel with the speculative Craft itself hence the lessons are inculcated in stages, or degrees, of initiation. The use of allegorical initiatory narratives, patterned on the quasi-historical circumstances surrounding the building of King Solomon's Temple and the metaphorical application of the Working Tools of operative stonemasonry, are examples of the indirect teaching methodology found in Freemasonry. It is through these esoteric, indirect approaches – as opposed to mere exoteric, superficial routes – that the material is conveyed, absorbed and thereby assimilated. Plus, to paraphrase Illustrious B. Albert Pike, the symbols of Freemasonry are meant to conceal as much to the *profanus* as they are to provide the impetus to contemplation for the initiate.[48] There is a synthesis which occurs when we meld empirical, experiential data with the powers of the intellect and the imagination in an initiatory rite that is simply unmatched by conventional modes of education. The initiatory experience is the essence of the Mystery Tradition; a tradition to which both Ceremonial Magick and Freemasonry belong.

> *Aristotle investigated both what happened in the minds of the audience at a tragedy and the experience offered by the annually recurring venture of Eleusis. The spectator at the tragedy had no need to build up a state of concentration by ritual preparations; he had no need to fast, to drink the kykeon [communion drink] and to march in a procession. He did not attain a state of epopteia, of "having seen" by his own inner resources. The poet, the chorus, the actors created a vision, the theama [spectacle], for him at the place designed for it, the teatron [theatre]. Without effort on his part, the spectator was transported into what he saw. What he saw and heard was made easy for him and became irresistibly his. He came to believe in it, but this belief was very different from that aroused by the epopteia [the vision of the Mysteries]. He [the spectator at the theatre] entered into other people's sufferings, forgot himself and—as Aristotle stressed— was purified. [But] in the Mysteries, a purification— katharmos—had to take effect long before the epopteia.[49]*

---

47   Jung, *Collected Works*, Vol. 14, Bollingen, 1968, pp. 654-668.
48   Pike, *Morals and Dogma*, L. H. Jenkins Inc., 1947, pp. 104-105.
49   Kerényi, *Eleusis: Archetypal Image of Mother and Daughter*, Bollingen, 1991, p. 113.

Variations on the grips, due guards and penal signs of the Masonic Lodge have been appropriated into the Golden Dawn and several post-Golden Dawn magical orders such as A∴A∴ and *Ordo Templi Orientis*. The performance of due guards and penal signs, in particular, have been extrapolated upon and used as a basis for God Forms, such as the LVX Signs.[50] The assumption of the God Forms was prescribed in these magical orders as a means of invoking the attributes of a mytho-theological archetype, such as that of Harpocrates who is invoked by giving the sign of silence, which is performed by placing the raised index finger to the center of the closed mouth. Though the relationship of the God Forms to their due guard and penal sign ancestors is somewhat obscured by innovation and customization, there are certain telltale verifications of their Masonic origins that would be imprudent to mention explicitly, but that any Mason would immediately detect.

Due to the invocative power of the practice, the Assumption of God Forms is a large part of the ritualism of several forms of Ceremonial Magick. The principal aim of this practice is the union of the individual consciousness with that of the archetypal entity.[51] Each god, or archetypal entity, is invoked by assuming a certain posture which hermetically identifies one with the entity whose characteristics one wishes to accentuate in one's own psyche. In this regard, the Assumption of God Forms functions as a psychic primer for more advanced operations such as attaining Knowledge and Conversation of the Holy Guardian Angel and Crossing the Abyss.[52] In psychoanalytic terms, these more advanced operations require the harnessing of the various archetypal forces within the magician's psyche which may be woven into a more complete and integrated expression of Self. Here, we again refer to the work of C.G Jung and his concept of individuation as a modern correlative to ideas present in Ceremonial Magick for over a century. As was stated above, the God Forms were obviously patterned on Masonic Due Guards and Penalty Signs, which were then fused with elements from the syncretization of several disparate culturo-mythological pantheons, such as the Egyptian, Assyro-Babylonian, Phoenician and Greco-Roman. This tendency to syncretization was very common theme in 20th century magical orders, particularly those based in hermetic qabalah.

---

50   Crowley, *Gems from the Equinox*, Weiser, 2007, p. 276.
51   Ibid. pp. 280-281.
52   Fortune, *The Mystical Qabalah*, Weiser, 1998, pp. 42-45.

Hand of the Mysteries

HERMETIC QABALAH AND SOLOMONIC MAGICK

In the supplementary literature and research surrounding Freemasonry's ritual and symbolism, one will periodically encounter references to kabbalah [kabbalah may be succinctly defined as: a mystical, Judaic, exegetical method and ontological schema, having its origins in medieval Europe]. This discipline is also explicitly referenced in certain degrees of the Masonic appendant body, the Ancient and Accepted Scottish Rite, and also in the Masonic invitational order, *Societas Rosicruciana*. When we consider kabbalah's association with Freemasonry, we are generally referring to the system's occult adaptation, commonly known within the Western Esoteric Tradition as hermetic qabalah. Hermetic qabalah is differentiated from Judaic kabbalah, and the Renaissance-era Christian cabala of Pico della Mirandola et al., primarily in its syncretization with hermeticism, astrology, alchemy, tarot symbolism and various mythologically archetypal elements from pagandom, particularly that of the Egyptian and Greco-Roman cultures. Hermetic qabalah is the form which was utilized by Freemasons such as Samuel Liddell MacGregor Mathers, William Wynn Westcott, Arthur Edward Waite (all members of the *Societas Rosicruciana* and its splinter group, the Hermetic Order of the Golden Dawn), Paul Foster Case (of the post-Golden Dawn orders, *Alpha et Omega* and the Builders of the Adytum) and Manly Palmer Hall (author of *The Secret Teachings of All Ages*, an encyclopedic compendium of the Western Esoteric Tradition).

The structure of 19th century Ceremonial Magick, essentially beginning with the work of Eliphas Levi, was erected on a foundation of hermetic qabalah.[53] Concurrently, and largely due to the scholarship of Ill. Bro. Albert Pike, the Ancient Accepted Scottish Rite of Freemasonry was infused with numerous overtly qabalistic references.[54] In fact, it has been conjectured that the 32 Degrees of the A.A.S.R. are esoterically related to the 32 paths on the *Etz Chaim*, or qabalistic Tree of Life.[55] Therein lays a primary and observable connection, in the company of several others less conspicuous, in terms of the various qabalistic tributaries which lead to both Ceremonial Magick and Freemasonry.

> *All truly dogmatic religions have issued from the Kabalah and return to it: everything scientific and grand in the religious dreams of all the illuminati, Jacob Boehme, Swedenborg, Saint-Martin, and others, is borrowed from the Kabalah; all the Masonic associations owe to it their Secrets and their Symbols.*[56]

Parallels have also been drawn between the Officer's stations, positioning of the Lodge furniture, the 'floor work' of ritual, and the compo-

---

53   Levi, *Transcendental Magic: Its Doctrine and Ritual*, Martino Publishing, 2011, p. 19.
54   Pike, *Morals and Dogma*, L. H. Jenkins Inc., 1947, pp. 744-745.
55   Hall, *The Secret Teachings of All Ages*, Dover, 2010, p. 333.
56   Levi, *Transcendental Magic: Its Doctrine and Ritual*, Martino Publishing, 2011, p. 19.

sition of Masonic tracing boards to certain *sephirothic* patterns on the *Etz Chaim*.[57] A more explicit example of these qabalistically derived patterns may be found in the Grade rituals of the Hermetic Order of the Golden Dawn, which openly make use of such configurations.[58] The Grades of the Golden Dawn, which correspond to the *sephiroth* of the *Etz Chaim*, are (in ascending order):

Neophyte 0=0
Zelator 1=10
Theoricus 2=9
Practicus 3=8
Philosophus 4=7
(Intermediate Portal Grade)
Ademptus Minor 5=6
Adeptus Major 6=5
Adeptus Exemptus 7=4
Magister Templi 8=3
Magus 9=2
Ipsissimus 10=1

These Grades were directly patterned on those of the Masonic *Societas Rosicruciana in Anglia*, which were themselves patterned on those of the *Orden des Gold und Rosenkreutz*, a Rosicrucian fraternity founded in 1750 by German Freemason and alchemist, Hermann Fichtuld. These Grades, in ascending order, were (corresponding and additional S.R.I.A. Grades in parentheses):

Juniorus (*Zelator*)
Theoricus
Practicus
Philosophus
Adeptus Minor
Adeptus Major
Adeptus Exemptus
Magister
Magus
(*Supreme Magus*)

---

57   MacNulty, *Kabbalah and Freemasonry* PDF, hayaryakanch.files.wordpress.com, 2015, retrieved online.
58   Regardie, *The Golden Dawn*, Llewellyn, 2014, p. 114.

The stations and movements of the officers and candidate, during the initiations of the Outer Order Grades of the Hermetic Order of the Golden Dawn, also follow qabalistic patterns that may choreographically be traced on the *Etz Chaim*.[59]

The *Etz Chaim* itself is primarily an ontological model in that it graphically depicts the qabalistic conception of (meta)physical manifestation and the intermediate stages of being, from *Ain*, or 'Nothing', to *Malkuth*, or 'Kingdom' which represents the material world. The diagram (below) also contains archetypal points along the segment in the form of the *sephiroth* (plural), or 'emanations', and the thirty-two Paths connecting them. Each *sephirah* (singular) is an archetypal placeholder, containing various mythological, astrological and hermetic correspondences. The *Etz Chaim*, and qabalism in general, is an integral component of the Western Hermetic Tradition and, as such, the use of this discipline as an interpretive tool is crucial to a well-rounded perspective of both Freemasonry and Ceremonial Magick. An in-depth exposition of qabalism – at least one that would do the topic justice – is outside of the scope of the present volume; however, many of the volumes in the bibliography of the present work are recommended for further qabalistic study.

---

59   Regardie, *The Golden Dawn*, Llewellyn, 2014, p. 115.

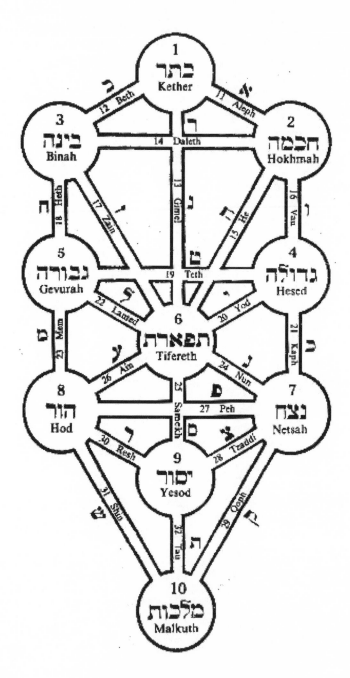

Etz Chaim – the qabalistic tree of life

Legends and narratives associated with King Solomon arise quite frequently in both Freemasonry and certain strains of Ceremonial Magick. Goetic Magick, which is based upon the *Ars Goetia* section of the 17th century grimoire *The Lesser Key of Solomon*[60], deals with the evocation of seventy-two daemons and their confinement in a brass vessel which was then sealed by magical sigils of King Solomon's creation. While the Blue Lodge makes use of the building of King Solomon's Temple as the setting for its allegorical rites, Goetic or Solomonic Magick understands King Solomon himself as the supreme Magus, wielding the power of these seventy-two daemons.[61] These spirits have been interpreted as concentrations of astrological influence whose zodiacal distributions are two per decan and six per house[62], thus dividing the ecliptic into seventy-two equal parts. Thereby further illustrating a hermetic sympathy by highlighting the correspondence between the celestial and terrestrial.[63] The very same daemons appear in the *One-Thousand and One (Arabian) Nights…*

> *Then he opened the meshes and found therein a cucumber-shaped jar of yellow copper, evidently full of something, whose mouth was made fast with a leaden cap, stamped with the seal-ring of our Lord Sulayman (Solomon) son of David (Allah accept the twain!). Seeing this the Fisherman rejoiced and said, 'If I sell it in the brass-bazaar, 'tis worth ten golden dinars.' He shook it and finding it heavy continued, 'Would to Heaven I knew what is herein. But I must and will open it and look to its contents and store it in my bag and sell it in the brass-market.' And taking out a knife he worked at the lead till he had loosened it from the jar; then he laid the cup on the ground and shook the vase to pour out whatever might be inside. He found nothing in it; whereat he marvelled with an exceeding marvel. But presently there came forth from the jar a smoke which spired heavenwards into æther (whereat he again marvelled with mighty marvel), and which trailed along earth's surface till presently, having reached its full height, the thick vapour condensed, and became an Ifrit, huge of bulk, whose crest touched the clouds while his feet were on*

---

60 Mathers/Crowley, *The Goetia*, Weiser, 1997, pp. xxiii-xxiv.
61 Ibid. pp. xxiii-xxiv.
62 Ibid. pp. 127-134.
63 See also: Mathers, *The Key of Solomon the King*, Weiser, 2006 and The Qur'an, Surah XXVII:15-18 for more about Solomon/Sulaiman and the Jinn (astro-elemental entities).

the ground. His head was as a dome, his hands like pitchforks,
his legs long as masts and his mouth big as a cave; his teeth
were like large stones, his nostrils ewers, his eyes two lamps
and his look was fierce and lowering. Now when the fisher-
man saw the Ifrit his side muscles quivered, his teeth chattered,
his spittle dried up and he became blind about what to do.
Upon this the Ifrit looked at him and cried, 'There is no god
but the God, and Sulayman is the prophet of God.'[64]

...and in the Qur'an[65], wherein they are referred to as *Jinn*, and are under the power of Sulayman (Solomon).

INITIATORY MYSTERIES

Many of the initiatory rites of modern magical orders are patterned on those of Freemasonry, just as the initiatory rites of Freemasonry have been surmised to be patterned on those of the Ancient Mysteries, such as Mithraism, Orphism and the Eleusinian Mysteries[66]. Consequently, we may thereby trace an observable and unifying lineage, based on the commonalities of their initiatory practices, of magical and Masonic initiation stretching back into the dawn of recorded history. In Masonic ritual, the candidate, being in an altered state of consciousness due to his experience in the Chamber of Reflection and the application of a *hoodwink* or blindfold, is conducted on his circumambulations about the Lodge room by the Senior Deacon, whose *psychopompic* role is archetypally reminiscent of that of *Herm-Anubis*.[67] The candidate is then instructed to "invoke the blessings of Deity". The fact that this constitutes an invocation is not in the least obscured. In this case, since this invocation is being performed amongst a group in open Lodge, the blessings may be considered to be those of the group's egregore (An autonomous psychic entity or thoughtform, usually representing a collective group mind), as opposed to any one individual's conception of a Supreme Being. This particular invocation is also another perfect example of magical theurgy in Masonic ritual, in that the interven-

---

64   *The Fisherman and the Jinni* from *The Arabian Nights*.
65   Qur'an, see Surahs XXVII and LXXII - both of which are numerically significant since there are seventy-two Djinn
66   Vail, *The Ancient Mysteries and Modern Masonry*, Forgotten Books, 2012, pp. 13-14.
67   New Larousse *Encyclopedia of Mythology*, Hamlyn Publishing Group, 1972, p. 123.

tion of the Supreme Being (or Egregore, in this case) is being requested to positively influence the initiatory process and the undertaking of the Work.

The act of circumambulation also delineates a sort of magic circle in which the operation at hand is to be worked.[68] The magic circle is used in several traditions of Natural and Ceremonial Magick. A space, within which the magical operation is to be performed, is delineated and consecrated. In a sense, the magic circle acts as an insulation which confines and condenses the energetic and/or psychic forces generated by the operation. This physical circumscription, as with those described with a pair of compasses, provides a magical focus of the will of the magician and a causal boundary of action.[69] The magic circle, in Masonry as in Ceremonial Magick, is almost exclusively traced *deosil*, or clockwise. The cardinal points of East, South and West (which are associated with the diurnal solar stages: dawn, midday and dusk) are then sequentially *passed* by the transmission of a word given by the Senior Deacon, on behalf of the initiate. This is akin to the demarcation of the cardinal points in the Golden Dawn's Lesser Ritual of the Pentagram, which we will discuss shortly.

As they pertain to a solar allegory, these three cardinal points represent the gates at which the protagonist was accosted by Three Ruffians (allegorically representing the Autumnal months) in the Hiramic Legend, with 'Low Twelve' functioning as a substitute for the North, which itself corresponds to the winter solstice[70] and the Underworld[71], be it the Duat or Hades. There is much evidence for the interpretation of the Hiramic Legend as the symbolic reenactment of the Sun's apparent annual circuit as seen from the perspective of the Earth[72] [73] – which again reinforces the hermetic, microcosm/macrocosm dynamic in Freemasonry. The Astro-mythological interpretation of Freemasonry's central allegory will be discussed in much further detail in Section II of this volume.

In some traditions of Ceremonial Magick, particularly those which were influenced by the work of Eliphas Levi[74], the cardinal points of East, South, West and North are zoomorphically represented as the ox, lion, eagle and man – otherwise known as the Tetramorph or the Four

68   Crowley, *Book 4, Part II*, Weiser, 2008, pp. 51-53.

69   Ibid., pp. 51-53.

70   Brown, *Stellar Theology and Masonic Astronomy*, Merchant Books, 2008, p. 43.

71   Higgins, *Hermetic Masonry*, Kessinger, 2012, p. 72.

72   Brown, *Stellar Theology and Masonic Astronomy*, Merchant Books, 2008, p. 43.

73   Hall, *The Secret Teachings of All Ages*, Dover, 2010, pp. 195-196.

74   Levi, *Transcendental Magic: Its Doctrine and Ritual*, Martino Publishing, 2011, p. 60.

Living Creatures of Ezekiel's Vision[75] and of John's Revelation.[76] These symbols are commonly thought to represent the zodiacal houses of Taurus, Leo, Scorpio (alternately, the Eagle or Phoenix) and Aquarius, respectively, but there are myriad other correspondences affixed to this quartet such as the Four Evangelists, the four Classical Elements, the equinoxes and solstices, the four suits of the Tarot and the letters of the Tetragrammaton, to name but a few.[77] [78] The Four Living Creatures, or Cherubim, are referenced heavily in many magical operations, the most common of which is the Lesser Ritual of the Pentagram.

The Cherubim of Ezekiel - Levi, *Transcendental Magic: Its Doctrine and Ritual*,
Martino, 2011, p. 161

75   *The Holy Bible*, Ezekiel 1:5-10.
76   Ibid. Revelation 4:7.
77   Regardie, *The Golden Dawn*, Llewellyn, 2014, p. 207.
78   Hall, *The Secret Teachings of All Ages*, Dover, 2010, p. 368.

The Lesser Ritual of the Pentagram (or, LRP – sometimes LBRP, for the banishing form, or LIRP, for the invoking) is an original ritual of the Hermetic Order of the Golden Dawn and, as such, was composed by Freemasons who were also members of the *Societas Rosicruciana in Anglia*. The LRP is a mainstay in modern Ceremonial Magick and occultism. This ritual functions as a preliminary clearing of the magician's working space and, simultaneously, as an evocation of the four Archangels (Raphael, Gabriel, Michael and Auriel) to act as sentinels at each of the cardinal points. It is generally begun with an appendant ritual called the Qabalistic Cross, which consists of the last few lines of *The Lord's Prayer*, recited in Hebrew, the construction of an astral cross, and the orienting of the magician within the *Etz Chaim* and vice-versa. Elemental pentagrams are then traced, either with the fingers or sometimes with an *athame*, or ceremonial dagger, while the names of God (YHVH, ADNI, AHIH) and the notariqon AGLA (a qabalistic acronym for *Atah Gibor Le-olam Adonai* – 'You, Oh Lord, are mighty forever') are intoned, or vibrated, at their corresponding cardinal direction. The ritual is then generally closed with another performance of the Qabalistic Cross. Within this ritual, certain visualizations are often generated – one of which is that of the Four Living Creatures.

> *Now, if thou wilt draw the Pentagram to have by thee as a symbol, thou shalt make it of the colours already taught, upon the black ground. There shall be the sign of the Pentagram, the Wheel, the Lion, the Eagle, the Ox, and the Man, and each hath an angle assigned unto it for dominion. Hence ariseth the Supreme Ritual of the Pentagram, according to the angle from which the Pentagram is traced. The circle or Wheel answereth to the all-pervading Spirit: The laborious Ox is the symbol of Earth; the Lion is the vehemence of Fire; the Eagle, the Water flying aloft as with wings when she is vaporized by the force of heat: the Man is the Air, subtle and thoughtful, penetrating hidden things.*[79]

In the Royal Arch Chapter of American Freemasonry, we find a representation of the *Tetramorph* depicted on the Royal Arch banner, whereupon they are flanked by two *androsphinxes* who are themselves emblematic of the solstices or Saints John, in the solar interpretation of the standard.[80] The Four Living Creatures are also referenced

79   Regardie, *The Golden Dawn*, Llewellyn, 2014, pp. 280.
80   Clark, *The Royal Secret*, Kessinger, 2012, pp. 129-130.

in the associated degree ceremony where they are attributed to the Judaic Tribes of Ephraim, Judah, Dan and Reuben. Not surprisingly, the *Tetramorph* also finds its way into the ritualism of the *Societas Rosicruciana* which, in addition to Levi's work, is likely where the founders of the Golden Dawn became aware of the quartet's magical import.

The Royal Arch Banner

In the second half of the Master Mason (or Third) Degree ceremony of Blue Lodge Freemasonry, the initiate experiences, in a first-person ritual drama, an elaborate allegorical rite resulting in the symbolic death and resurrection of an archetypal subdivision of his own psyche. The initiate, through a series of events and actions, becomes the symbolic host to the 'Light Body'[81] or spirit of the quasi-historical, mythic persona of one

---

81   Levi, *Transcendental Magic: Its Doctrine and Ritual*, Martino Publishing, 2011, p. 66 and elsewhere regarding *Azoth* and Levi's concept of the Astral Light.

Hiram Abiff. Hiram Abiff – being the central figure in the most significant Masonic allegory: the Hiramic Legend – has inhabited the imagination and psyche of every Master Mason to such an extent that one might
say that his persona has become egregorically realized in the collective
consciousness of Freemasonry. Through the identification with this entity,
while being psychologically subjected to the events in narrative, the astral
consciousness of Hiram Abiff is evoked into the host/initiate.[82] The associations that cling to this persona, while it is subjectively inhabiting the
initiate's psyche, are effectively killed and then resurrected into a more per-
fected form that is no longer subject to physical death. At the culmination
of this ceremony, when the application three grips serve as the keys to *raise*
the initiate from his previous condition into his new station, it is difficult
for the candidate to doubt those three integral Masonic tenets: *the Father-
hood of God, the Brotherhood of Man and the Immortality of the Human Soul.*

In this context, Masonic ritual functions as a sort of magical prax-
is even in the life of a Mason with no conscious or pre-existing occult or
esoteric inclination. That is to say that, theoretically, the individual Mason
need not be conscious of the terms of a particular magical equation but, if
he is subject to the working itself, then he must necessarily be subliminally
affected by it. The objective efficacy of the initiatory experience has made
this evident – hence the tendency of most cultures, since time immemorial, to utilize this form of social transformation. It is expected to be the
case that the candidate for the Mysteries of Freemasonry has no empirical
data regarding his initiation before he is initiated – his awareness is therefore heightened, his senses keen, because knows not what to expect. He is
then subjected to a sequence of events which effectively constitute a very
deliberate magical working, leaving the initiate irrevocably transformed
from a one state or degree of existence to another through a liminal rite of
passage. This transformation, which takes place on a psycho-mythological
level, and the accompanying paradigm shift is effected by the initiatory
experience itself. The *medium* does, indeed, contain the *message*. The candidate reaps the sublime benefit of initiatory degree conferral by synthesiz-
ing the rational and the mystical; by integrating the Sun and the Moon;
by officiating the hermetic marriage. Had he been sat down in a room and
simply told the lessons, secrets and Mysteries inculcated in the ceremonies
of his initiation – however profound their metaphysical import – these
lessons would have remained mere tidbits of intellectual data, devoid of the
sort of subconscious penetration necessary to achieve a deep absorption of
the material. Conversely, had he been subjected to a fantastical cloud of

---

82   Ibid., pp. 119-121.

meaningless abstractions, emptied of any real-world application or practical frame of reference (such as the nihilistic obliteration of the ego, or the buddhistic negation of the Will; and other typically Eastern and 'New Age-y' notions that seem to be antithetical to individuation and self-actualization), he would be able to gain no foothold in his lofty ascent. These two tendencies, which have been reflected in nearly every occult, magical and Masonic dichotomy, must be integrated to form a coherent and unified picture of microcosmic Man in the macrocosmic Universe.

As we have seen, Freemasonry and Ceremonial Magick make use of a strikingly similar body of symbolism, ritualism and allegorical content. Moreover, we have shown that both traditions utilize conditioned, or ceremonially prepared, states of consciousness to bypass purely cerebral interpretations of said ritual and symbolism. This initiatory methodology seems to enable a more profound penetration into the deeper recesses of the psyche, thereby allowing the initiate to gain access to those hazy archetypal elements which have been associated with the collective unconscious. A similar phenomenon has been noted to occur in many rites of passage across many ages and cultures. In several strains of Ceremonial Magick, this initiatory phenomenon is said to find its fruition in the Knowledge and Conversation of the Holy Guardian Angel, which is akin to other states of being, such as individuation, self-realization and gnosis – wherein 'subject and object become *one* in the act of knowing'.[83]

THE EFFECT OF MITHRAISM ON FREEMASONRY AND CEREMONIAL MAGICK

Aside from Freemasonry's aforementioned connections to the magical orders of the late 19th and early 20th centuries, and the generous tributaries of hermeticism and qabalism, both of which we have investigated, there exists a compelling argument for the influence of Mithraism on the structure and substance of Freemasonry and, thereby, on that of Ceremonial Magick.

Mithraism was a Roman Mystery religion, replete with an initiatory Grade system. What we know of Mithraism comes to us mainly due to the religion's prestigious station as the preferred cult of the Roman Legionaries.[84] Numerous *mithraea* (singular, *mithraeum* – the temple-grottoes in

---

83   Wilbur, *Quantum Questions: Mystical Writings of the World's Great Physicists,* Shambhala, 2001, p. 4.
84   Geden, *Select Passages Illustrating Mithraism,* Kessinger, p. 51.

which their Mysteries were conferred), bas-reliefs and statuary still pepper the former Roman Empire. It is believed that, at the religion's height, there were almost seven-hundred of these temples spread across the Empire; four-hundred-and-twenty of these sites have been excavated thus far.

Speculum Romanae Magnificentiae, Special Collections Research Center, University of Chicago Library

Adherents to the earlier forms of Persian mysticism that birthed the theological, philosophical, and astrological systems that would become Mithraism were called *magi*, which is the etymological root of the word *magic.*[85] The Latin singular form for *magi* is *magus*, which has made several appearances as a Grade appellation in various Rosicrucian and hermetic orders, notably the Masonic invitational order *Societas Rosicruciana*, founded in the mid-19th Century.

Like the Magician's Temple and the Masonic Lodge, the Mithraic grotto was known to be a microcosmic representation of the Universe and, similarly, there are many signs and symbols of a generally astrological character, such as those associated with the grades and the astrological interpretation of the *Tauroctony*, which will be discussed in Section II of this volume.

> *In the Mysteries of Mithras, a sacred cave, representing the whole arrangement of the world, was used for the reception of the Initiates. Zoroaster, says Eubulus, first introduced this custom of consecrating caves. They were also consecrated, in Crete, to Jupiter; in Arcadia, to the Moon and Pan; and in the Island of Naxos, to Bacchus. The Persians, in the cave where the Mysteries of Mithras were celebrated, fixed the seat of that God, Father of Generation, or Demiourgos, near the equinoctial point of Spring, with the Northern portion of the world on his right, and the Southern on his left.*[86]

Additionally, the Mithraic Grade structure was sometimes represented by a seven-runged ladder which also corresponded to the seven classical planets and the seven alchemical metals.[87] [88] This, of course, finds a parallel in the Masonic Lodge in the often-present representation of Jacob's Ladder, the rungs of which have been attributed to some of the same correspondences.

This is, by no means, an exhaustive account of the many correlations that illuminate the magical current culturally uniting ancient Persian Magism with Ceremonial Magick, but it will suffice to illustrate the point. We have also seen that Roman Mithraism and Freemasonry are not mere links in the chain of lineage but that they have additionally served as contributing influences to the organic development of modern Ceremonial Magick.

85　　Online Etymology Dictionary, etymonline.com, retrieved 2015.

86　　Pike, *Morals and Dogma*, L. H. Jenkins Inc., 1947, p. 413.

87　　Mackey, The Symbolism of Freemasonry, Forgotten Books, 2012, p. 342.

88　　Pike, *Morals and Dogma*, L. H. Jenkins Inc., 1947, p. 11.

CONCLUSION OF SECTION I

Freemasonry is not only replete with an inherent capacity for those mystical qualities which characterize Ceremonial Magick, but it has served as a faithful depository for much of the magical arcana of the Western World, in general. Its structure has served as sort of filing cabinet – one containing samples from nearly all ages and traditions of ritualism and symbolism – from which the formal model and initial components for numerous magical and mystical orders has subsequently been borrowed.

Ceremonial Magick has benefited much from its adoption of Masonic structure and systemization. This association has allowed for a coherent and workable classification for a myriad of ritual systems found throughout the Western World. The formal qualities present in Freemasonry also provide the magical practitioner with a broad, intuitive framework that fittingly lends itself to the working of all manner of magical operations, particularly those involving rite and ceremony.

Again, Freemasonry and Ceremonial Magick are not merely complimentary traditions but, because their synergetic relationship is an integral and indispensable component of each system, one could simply not exist in its current form without the other. Freemasonry and Ceremonial Magick are parallel systems with a high potential for further integration, even if only through their employment in the practice of an individual. These two seemingly discrete traditions have enjoyed a protracted period of cross-fertilization, which has proven to be mutually advantageous in that the development of each, as we have shown, has clearly informed the other. Furthermore, there is no apparent reason to suspect that these ancient traditions, which have shared so much throughout their respective histories, will not remain mutually influential going forward.

SECTION II:

SOLAR AND ASTROLOGICAL SYMBOLISM IN FREEMASONRY

SOLAR AND ASTROLOGICAL SYMBOLISM IN FREEMASONRY

"[...] the masonic tradition is but one of the numerous ancient allegories of the yearly passage of the personified Sun among the twelve constellations of the zodiac — being founded on a system of astronomical symbols and emblems employed for the purpose of teaching and illustrating the two great truths, of the being of One, spiritual, omnipresent, and omnipotent God and the immortality of the soul of man."[1]

Of all the known symbolic and allegorical themes in Western Civilization, none are more ubiquitous than those that, when reduced to their root narrative, pertain to the movement of celestial bodies, particularly the apparent annual and diurnal circuits of the Sun. This is unsurprising, considering the importance of the role of this star in maintaining life on Earth. To the ancients, as to modern man, nothing was more observably significant, in its presence or its absence, than the light and heat provided by this fiery orb. The Sun's apparent path measures the passage of time; its relative position to the Earth marks the changing of seasons. The solar cycle pervades nearly every aspect of human life and civilization. The Sun was, is, and presumably will continue to be, temporal reference point number one.

The Sun's passage across the ecliptic and through the twelve houses of the zodiac has provided the framework for numberless mythological narratives, allegory, fable, and folklore. This solar/astrological influence is also present in the rituals and symbolism of Freemasonry; though it is so ingeniously woven into the fabric of the Fraternity that it often escapes notice. It is the purpose of the present work to attempt to illustrate, through the application of an astrological interpretation of the material inherent in Freemasonry's ritualistic and diagrammatic corpus, that this ancient fraternal order has functioned as a repository for a body

---

1   Robert Hewitt Brown, *Stellar Theology and Masonic Astronomy*, Merchant Books, 2008, p. 16.

of symbolism and allegory that is astrological in general, and solar in particular, and thereby modern Freemasonry continues to per-
petuate an element common to many ancient Mystery Traditions.

ASTROLOGY AND ASTRONOMY

Being that we are approaching this subject with an emphasis on astrological symbolism, it is necessary that we first differentiate astrology
from astronomy. These disciplines are similar in that both measure and
chronicle the various movements and relative positions of celestial bodies. Astronomy accomplishes this by means of detailed mathematical and
astrophysical calculations.[2] Astrology, however, is distinguished by the accompanying belief that these motions and cycles have a psychological and
physiological influence on human beings[3], thus the sympathetic relationship between the microcosm and the macrocosm is a necessary and defin-
ing factor of this hermetic art. It is also worth considering that astrology
and astronomy share the same operative/speculative dynamic that is found
between alchemy and chemistry, and between accepted freemasonry and
physical stonemasonry.

It is pertinent, particularly from a Masonic standpoint, to bear in
mind as we go forward that Astronomy is, of course, one of the Seven Liberal Arts and Sciences, occupying the maximal position in the *Quadrivium*.
The *Quadrivium* itself is sequentially ordered in that it begins with arithmetic (abstract numerical operations), then to geometry (number in fixed
space), music (number in time) and reaches its completion in astronomy
(number in space-time), which utilizes and unifies the preceding three disciplines.

---

2   Dictionary, *Merriam Webster*, retrieved online.
3   Ibid., retrieved online.

Zodiac, Barocius, 1585

ASTROLOGY IN THE WESTERN MYSTERY TRADITIONS

When we refer to the Mystery Traditions of the ancient world, we are referring specifically to those institutions and orders whose primary function was to serve as depositories for the accumulated metaphysics of the given culture, and to judiciously disseminate occult doctrines via the medium of initiation, which were generally organized in hierarchical grades or degrees.[4] These institutions were often distinguished from their corresponding civil religions by rites of initiation and oaths of secrecy, and consequently very little information has made it to us directly as to the specific nature and structure of these orders. However, from the data that has been gathered via archeological fragments and artifacts, a good deal of the curricula of these schools, as well as insights into their theological and

4   Vail, *The Ancient Mysteries and Modern Masonry*, Forgotten Books, 2012, pp. 13-19.

philosophical pursuits, may be deduced with some confidence. The accumulated arts and sciences that are generally presumed to have been in the keeping of these orders included the preservation of the culture's ritualistic and magical heritage, cosmological and eschatological Mysteries, the secrets of agriculture, the crafts of architecture and construction, shamanic and/or entheobotanical medicine, and the methods of astronomical observation.[5] It is Masonically notable that several of these arts and sciences are predicated on a familiarity with geometry. By using allegories and parables, in conjunction with various symbolic and mnemonic devices, knowledge of these various processes was conveyed, often via the medium of ritualized drama.

Like civilization itself, many of the Mystery Traditions were presumed to be established initially upon an agricultural foundation. The prediction, speculation, calculation and even the taxation of agricultural prospects and commodities was predicated on an understanding of arithmetic, geometry and, perhaps above all, astronomical observation. The safeguarding of the accumulated practical and theoretical knowledge of these sciences was of extreme importance; and it is for this reason that this body of information was consequently deposited in the bosom, or 'faithful breast', of the Mysteries, where oaths of silence and fidelity would ensure the maintenance of its integrity.

Communication of the mysteries via solar allegories was relatively common within many of the agricultural Mystery Religions of the ancient world.[6] The overall sequence of these rites helped to illustrate seasonal cycles, which was crucial knowledge for farming and cultivation, in addition to the set of metaphysical conclusions professed by the particular sect. Initiation into this type of Mystery Cult generally consisted of an exemplar for the region's solar personification of choice whose passage through the twelve houses of the zodiac in one annual circuit was dramatically rendered.[7] Though the practical import of those ritual-dramas which allegorized the annual solar circuit was largely agricultural, there was usually a mystical component that centered on concepts such as cosmology, eschatology, immortality and metempsychosis, or the transmigration of the human soul into another form at death. These metaphysical Mysteries often employed concoctions derived from regional plant entheogens.

---

5   Higgins, *Hermetic Masonry*, Kessinger, 2012, pp. 14-15.
6   Clark, *The Royal Secret*, Kessinger, 2012, pp. 4-5.
7   Vail, *The Ancient Mysteries and Modern Masonry*, Forgotten Books, 2012, pp. 38-60.

THE RELEVANCE OF MITHRAIC ASTROLOGICAL SYMBOLISM IN FREEMASONRY

Mithraism was a popular Mystery Religion among the Roman Legionaries[8] having its origins in 4th Century BCE Persian Zoroastrianism. As discussed in Section I, the *mithraea*, like Masonic Lodge rooms, were said to be microcosmic representations of the Universe. For example, traces of blue paint, understood to have been used in the recreation of the night sky, have been found on the ceiling of the *Caesarea Maritima Mithraeum*.[9] The Mithraic Grade structure was sometimes represented by a seven-runged ladder which also corresponded to the seven classical planets – the Sun, Moon, Mercury, Mars, Venus, Jupiter and Saturn – those which were visible to the ancients, prior to the invention of the telescope. A parallel could also be drawn here with the Masonic adoption of the symbolism of Jacob's Ladder, in terms of a celestial ascent. "In the Mithraic ceremonies," said Pike, "the candidate went through seven stages of initiation, passing through many fearful trials – and of these the high ladder with seven rounds or steps was the symbol."[10] The grades of Mithraism are believed to have been as follows (listed here, in ascending order, with their translations and corresponding planetary influences):

Corax (crow, Mercury)
Nymphus (bridegroom, Venus)
Miles (soldier, Mars)
Leo (lion, Jupiter)
Perses (Persian, Luna)
Heliodromus (sun-runner, Sol)
Pater (father, Saturn)

The first *Anno Lucis* of Freemasonry, when calculated by the cycles of axial precession, would have occurred in proximity to the dawn of the Taurian Age[11] (The period of about 2160 years that the vernal equinox occurred within the 30 degrees of the ecliptic referred to as zodiacal house of Taurus), which spanned from approximately 4000 – 2000

---

8   Graves, *The White Goddess*, FSG Classics, 2013, p. 204.
9   Hopfe, *Archaeological indications on the origins of Roman Mithraism*, Rosicrucian Digest No. 2, AMORC, 2008, p. 21.
10   Pike, *Morals and Dogma*, L. H. Jenkins Inc., 1947, p. 11.
11   Hancock, *Fingerprints of the Gods*, Three Rivers, 1995, pp. 238-241.

BCE. Mithraism is laden with Taurian imagery, as evidenced in nearly every known grotto. It has been suggested that the *Tauroctony* – a depiction of Mithras as a solar personification, surmounting and slaying a bull – is a symbolic representation of the vernal equinox occurring in the house of Taurus, thus harkening back to the very same period as that of the Masonic *Anno Lucis*. In the *Tauroctony*, on either side of Mithras and the Taurian Bull, there are depictions of the torchbearers Cautes and Cautopates. These characters, cross-legged and dressed in distinctly Anatolian garb, have been interpreted as representations of the solstices[12], as have the Saints John via the two parallel, perpendicular lines – one ascribed with a letter *B* for John the Baptist and the other with a letter *E* for John the Evangelist – in the Masonic Point Within A Circle diagram. Cautes and Cautopates are also reminiscent of the solstitial *androsphinxes* who flank the *Tetramorph* on the Royal Arch banner, as discussed in Section I.

> *Mithras, says Porphyry, presided over the Equinoxes, seated on a Bull, the symbolical animal of the Demiourgos, and bearing a sword. The equinoxes were the gates through which souls passed to and fro, between the hemisphere of light and that or darkness. The milky way was also represented, passing near each of these gates: and it was, in the old theology, termed the pathway of souls. It is, according to Pythagoras, vast troops of souls that form that luminous belt.[13]*

The Mithraic Grade of *Miles* is believed to have consisted of the performance of an annual solar circuit represented in an allegorized ritual-drama. During this ritual, the initiate was said to descend into the grotto via the gate of Cancer (representing the summer solstice – which is notable as an annual correlative to the diurnal 'High Twelve' of Freemasonry and also to the Keystone position of the Royal Arch in Capitular Masonry), where he passed through the spheres of the seven classical planets. Upon his descent into this chthonic realm, the *Miles*, after having adopted a quality of each planetary sphere through which he had passed, was subjected to the judgement of Mithras. He was then purged of the qualities he had collected during his descent by the performance of seven sacraments and made his exit via the gate of Capricorn (the winter sol-

---

12   Ruck, Hoffman and Celdran, *Mushrooms, Myths and Mithras*, City Lights, 2011, p. 60.
13   Pike, *Morals and Dogma*, L. H. Jenkins Inc., 1947, p. 413.

stice, or 'Low Twelve' in the Masonic analogy). Also, in the initiatory rite known as the 'Procession of the Sun Runner', the *Heliodromus* is guided by *Cautes* and *Cautopates* and preceded by an initiate of the *Miles* Grade in a ritual circumambulation about the *mithraeum*, allegorically representing an annual solar circuit.[14] Similarly, a guided circumambulation in a *deosil*, or clockwise, direction is also performed in Masonic initiations. An allegorically solar interpretation has also been applied, very compellingly, to the Hiramic Legend in Masonic ritual,[15] which will be discussed in greater detail toward the end of the present Section.

THE HERMETIC SYMPATHY BETWEEN THE MICROCOSM AND THE MACROCOSM

Hermeticism pertains, primarily, to the study and practice of the doctrines attributed to Hermes Trismegistus.[16] These doctrines come to us via discovered fragments which have been compiled in what is known as the *Corpus Hermeticum*. Among the tracts which constitute this corpus is the *Tabula Smaragdina*, also known as *The Emerald Tablet of Hermes*. This notable piece of hermetica, widely considered to be largely alchemical in nature, is the source of the axiom: "that which is above is like that which is below."[17] This axiom, which has been represented in more recent times as the Hermetic Principle of Correspondence[18], has been applied, interpretatively, to the celestial orientation of terrestrial structures. There are many examples – from the megalithic structures of the Neolithic Era, through the cathedrals of the medieval Period, to many modern edifices – of astronomical alignments and astrological allusions, particularly as they pertain to the equinoxes and solstices and, more specifically, the phenomenon of axial precession.

---

14   Martin, *Ritual Competence and Mithraic Ritual,* 2004, p. 257.
15   Brown, *Stellar Theology and Masonic Astronomy,* Merchant Books, 2008, pp. 43–44.
16   Barnstone and Meyer (editors), *The Gnostic Bible,* Shambhala, 2009, pp. 517-518.
17   Hall, *The Secret Teachings of All Ages,* Dover, 2010, pp. 454-457.
18   Three Initiates, *The Kybalion,* Kessinger, 2012, p. 5.

The Emerald Tablet - Kunrath, *Amphitheatrum Sapientiæ Æternæ*, Hanau, 1609

Freemasonry's observance of the sympathetic relationship between the microcosm and the macrocosm is demonstrated in several ways. The orientation and design of the Lodge room is plainly stated to be a model of the Universe.[19] Much of the 'floor work' of the Lodge officers, particularly the act of circumambulation, has been conjectured to be a hermetic imitation of the Sun's apparent path along the ecliptic as viewed from the perspective of the Earth.[20] The Terrestrial and Celestial Globes surmounting the Pillars of the Temple also reflect a similar correspondence.[21] Additionally, Freemasonry's initiatory dramatizations, particularly those of a solar or otherwise astronomical nature, clearly fit this description if we apply the appropriate interpretive keys.[22]

---

19   Mackey, *The Symbolism of Freemasonry*, Forgotten Books, 2012, pp. 100-105.
20   Brown, *Stellar Theology and Masonic Astronomy*, Merchant Books, 2008, p. 59.
21   Clark, *The Royal Secret*, Kessinger, 2012, p. 103.
22   Brown, *Stellar Theology and Masonic Astronomy*, Merchant Books, 2008, pp. 43-44.

FREEMASONRY'S RELATIONSHIP TO ASTRONOMY

Throughout Freemasonry's initiatory degrees and the accompanying lectures, explanations of the various sets of symbols are given. These lectures and explanations primarily focus on the moral and ethical interpretations of said symbols. However, there are several alternate interpretations that may be applied to Masonic ritual and symbolism to great effect. These interpretations yield a deeper insight into the Fraternity's wide range of inspirations and the influences with which the Craft has been imbued, in addition to providing a foothold for metaphysical contemplation. Among these alternate interpretive keys are the solar and astrological. Freemasonry abounds with allusions to various celestial objects and phenomena in addition to allegorical content, unique to Masonic ritual, which can be understood to represent cycles such as the annual and diurnal solar circuits, planetary orbits and even axial precession.

As we have discussed in Section I, there is a distinction made in Freemasonry between the operative and the speculative Crafts. The beginnings of operative Masonry can be seen as early as the Neolithic Era.[23] It is here that we begin to see the earliest examples of edifices composed of quarried and worked stone. Many of these early structures betray an inordinately high level of geometrical and astronomical proficiency, particularly when considered in the context of the accepted cultural development of the period. When the application of geometrical principles in architecture becomes apparent, we can begin to trace the operative origins of Freemasonry; most clearly evidenced by the conception and execution of megalithic structures in prehistory. Many of these edifices were oriented to astronomical events such as the solstices and equinoxes, serving to further establish that these structures were conceived and raised in keeping with the aforementioned hermetic principles.

We must then further consider the fact that this information was limited to the class of the architect and builder, among whom these practices had become trade secrets.[24] That these masons, with the probable addition of the priestly class or hierophants of the Mysteries, were in possession of the astrological keys that yielded the science of geometry (and the arts dependent upon it) is incontrovertible when considered in view of their work. Thus we see the gradual stratification of a class of craftsmen who had designed and erected these ancient and astronomically-oriented structures

---

23   Scham, *The World's First Temple*, Archaeology Magazine, Dec. 2008, p. 23.
24   Mackey, *The Symbolism of Freemasonry*, Forgotten Books, 2012, pp. 47-48.

in stone, many notable examples of which remain standing to this day, which is itself a physical testament to the quality of their workmanship.

The word *geometry* has its etymological root in the Ancient Greek γεωμετρία. That the word itself is in reference to the measurement (*metron*) of the Earth (*geo*) is significant to our subject in that the only means by which the topography of the Earth may be terrestrially measured is in juxtaposition to the celestial sphere. Otherwise, the process of Earth measurement would be akin to measuring a ruler with the same ruler – one will always arrive at a 1:1 ratio. Bearing this in mind, it is difficult to say, conclusively, if the science of astronomy is dependent upon geometry, as it is inferred in a Lodge of Fellowcraft Masons, or whether geometry is, itself, an abstraction drawn from astronomical observation.

By marking the solstices, equinoxes and stellar phenomena, mankind gradually became able to gain a sense of space, time and the rhythms of the Earth. By extrapolating the accumulated data and the procedures used in the observance of astronomical events, he was able to apply this knowledge to other areas such as agriculture, navigation and architecture – i.e. the arts and sciences upon which human civilization is contingent.

ASTRONOMICAL ORIENTATION IN MEDIEVAL CATHEDRAL BUILDING

The fact that innumerable edifices, dating from the Neolithic Era through the Middle Ages and into the present day, have been conceived and erected with the express purpose of hermetically mirroring astronomical formations is irrefutable. Archeologists continue to find structures widely distributed over the surface of the Earth that betray the telltale signs of astronomical orientation.[25] Due to these considerations, we can safely infer that many of the temples of the ancient world were used for ritualistic as well as observatorial purposes, such as marking agricultural cycles and highlighting solstitial and equinoctial events.

Some of the early known guilds of stonemasons, such as the Dionysian Artificers and the Roman *Collegia*, were likely to have perpetuated not only the trade secrets of the operative Craft, but also some of the arcana which would have been inculcated in several of the ancient Mystery Traditions.[26] This may account for the undiluted and undiffused transmission

---

25　　Hiebert, *Celestial and Mathematical Precision in Ancient Architecture*, University of Manitoba, World-Mysteries.com, retrieved online.

26　　Mackey, *The History of Freemasonry*, Kessinger, 2012, pp. 166-173.

of the requisite practical and theoretical knowledge of geometry and astronomy necessary for the construction of the sort of celestially-aligned structures that we find.

> *However, it is more than a mere plausible inference that from the beginning architects were members of secret orders; for, as we have seen, not only the truths of religion and philosophy, but also the facts of science and the laws of art, were held as secrets to be known only to the few. This was so, apparently without exception, among all ancient peoples; so much so, indeed, that we may take it as certain that the builders of old time were initiates. Of necessity, then, the arts of the craft were secrets jealously guarded, and the architects themselves, while they may have employed and trained ordinary workmen, were men of learning and influence.[27]*

Chartres Cathedral, west portal zodiac and monthly labors

Later, the Lombard stonemasons of the Middle Ages, such as the *Magistri Comacini* and the *Maestri Campionesi*, represented a continuation of these concerns in the operative Craft. The esoteric import embedded in

27   Newton, *The Builders*, 1914, pp. 73-74, retrieved online at sacred-texts.com.

the pedagogical culture of these guilds is readily made apparent when one considers the symbolism employed in edifices such as Chartres Cathedral in France...

> *The structure of the labyrinth in the Cathedral at Char-*
> *tres points to its possible and probable use for astronomical*
> *demonstrations and calculations. The numbers and geometry*
> *involved may clarify the fundamentals of celestial mechanics*
> *from the geocentric viewpoint consistent with twelfth centu-*
> *ry knowledge as well as the performance of the computus for*
> *determining the date of Easter and all moveable feasts of the*
> *liturgical year. Using an algorithm based on Bede's De tem-*
> *porum ratione (The Reckoning of Time) real people or pawns*
> *may be moved on the labyrinth itself, or on a small or imag-*
> *inary replica of it, to calculate the date of Easter. It might*
> *have therefore been used as an educational tool at the School of*
> *Chartres in the early thirteenth century for teaching astron-*
> *omy and mathematics besides the liturgical, mnemotechnical*
> *and spiritual usages that we will explore elsewhere.*[28]

... and Rosslyn Chapel in Scotland...

> *The planners and builders of Rosslyn Chapel were skilled as-*
> *tronomers and understood the Julian calendar and its failings*
> *very well. They therefore oriented the chapel to the part of the*
> *horizon it should face, irrespective of the incorrect nature of the*
> *calendar in the 15th century.*[29]

These are but two of many structures around the globe which bear the indelible stamp of astronomical orientation and allusions to other celestial phenomena through the spatial utilization of number and proportion – not to mention the presence of copious examples of overtly paganistic imagery – and it is important to bear in mind, as it directly pertains to our subject, that these edifices were unquestionably constructed by operative stonemasons.

---

28   LeMee, *Chartres Cathedral Studies*, 2013, retrieved online.
29   Butler and Ritchie, *Rosslyn Chapel Decoded: New Interpretations of a Gothic Enigma*, Watkins Media Ltd, 2012, PDF retrieved online.

EXAMPLES OF SOLAR AND ASTROLOGICAL
SYMBOLISM IN FREEMASONRY

As was previously stated, it is the purpose of this Section of the present work to illuminate the significance of some of the less conspicuous astrological inferences and allusions occurring in Freemasonry's diagrammatic content, banners, standards, insignia, regalia, jewels, Lodge room, modes of recognition and in nearly every aspect of the Craft's ritual and degree work. Considering that it would be nearly impossible to exhaustively catalog every instance of possible astrological import, the following will be limited to a few of the more illustrative examples, yet it is hoped that this general overview will inspire the inquisitive Mason to pursue further light in this exceedingly fruitful area of research.

THE ANNO LUCIS AND AXIAL PRECESSION

The *Anno Lucis* (Latin, 'Year of Light') is a symbolic dating system peculiar to Freemasonry. Often abbreviated as A.L., this dating method is frequently used on Masonic cornerstones and documentation. The *Anno Lucis* adds 4000 years to the Common Era dating system and is a simplification of the *Anno Mundi*, which adds 4004 years to the *Anno Domini*, to which the act of Creation was attributed in the Masoretic text.[30] When this date is utilized as a temporal vantage point from which to survey Masonic ritual and symbolism, we begin to realize the value of the *Anno Lucis* as an interpretive key.

A working knowledge of the movement of celestial bodies was, and continues to be, of the utmost importance to agricultural civilization. Indeed, it was often a matter of life or death – or, more accurately, feast or famine. It was in light of the importance placed upon this study that early astronomers began to catalog the various stellar and planetary cycles. It is necessary that we take a moment to develop a basic conception, in the absence of detailed astrophysical calculations, of axial precession, as the astrological interpretation of some of the subsequent material is predicated upon such an understanding.

Also known as the 'Precession of the Equinoxes', axial precession was

---

30   Mendoza, *Ars Quatuor Coronatorum, the Transactions of Quatuor Coronati Lodge No. 2076*, UGLE, Volume 95, http://freemasonry.bcy.ca, 1980, retrieved online.

said to have first been discerned by the 2nd Century BCE astronomer, Hipparchus of Rhodes; however, there are many earlier examples that allude to a knowledge of this phenomenon that have yet to be substantiated.[31] Axial precession has been defined as the slow and continuous change in orientation of a celestial body on its rotational axis due to the gravitational influence of adjacent bodies.[32] From the perspective of the Earth, the zodiacal belt appears to go in reverse during this cycle, hence the term *precession*. One complete cycle, through all twelve zodiacal houses, i.e. 360 degrees, takes approximately 25,920 years. This is known, alternately, as the Great, or Platonic Year. Due to precession, every zodiacal house has hosted the Earth's vernal equinox. The approximately 2160 year period in which the vernal equinox occurs in a particular house is referred to as a precessional age.[33] We are currently on the cusp of the Piscean and Aquarian Ages. Since the Neolithic Era, in which we see the beginnings of settled civilization – which was largely due to developments in agriculture and animal husbandry – mankind has seen the passage of several precessional ages. This phenomenon, in addition to other astronomical events, has influenced the body of symbolism created and collected by every ancient civilization of which we are aware. These symbolic allusions may also be found in great number in Freemasonry, as we will investigate in the following.

31   Hiebert, *Celestial and Mathematical Precision in Ancient Architecture*, University of Manitoba, World-Mysteries.com, retrieved online.
32   Hohenkerk, Yallop, Smith and Sinclair, *Explanatory Supplement to the Astronomical Almanac*, University Science Books, p. 99.
33   Hancock, *Fingerprints of the Gods*, Three Rivers, 1995, pp. 232-237.

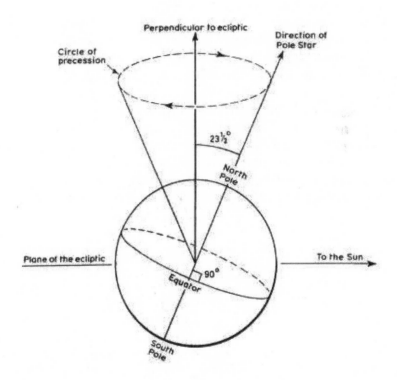

Axial precession is the wobbling of the Earth's North/South axis over a period of approximately 25,920 years – a cycle which causes the vernal equinox to occur in each zodiacal house for a period of about 2160 years and, when complete, constitutes one Great or Platonic Year

THE FIXED SIGNS OF THE ZODIAC

In astrology, both modern and ancient, the twelve houses of the zodiac are divided into quadruplicities, or three groups each containing four signs.[34] These groups divide the cardinal, fixed and mutable signs. The cardinal signs are Aries, Cancer, Libra and Capricorn. The fixed signs are Leo, Scorpio, Aquarius and Taurus. The mutable signs are Sagittarius, Pisces, Gemini and Virgo. The four signs contained in each group equally quarter the zodiacal belt so, due to this configuration, when the vernal equinox occurs in a cardinal sign, for example, the summer solstice, autumnal equinox and the winter solstice will also occur in a cardinal sign. This alignment phenomenon likewise occurs in the fixed and mutable quadruplicities.

Bearing this in mind, if one were to wind the 'precessional clock' back to the Taurian Age, i.e. commencing from approximately 4000 BCE and terminating around 2000 BCE, one would observe the equinoxes and solstices inhabiting the fixed signs: Taurus, Leo, Scorpio (anciently conflated with the eagle or phoenix) and Aquarius (generally rendered as a man). This astrological quartet, whose most notable appearances are as the *Cherubim* in Ezekiel's Vision[35] and as the Four Living Creatures in John's Vision[36], has been frequently depicted in religious visual art, bas-relief and statuary.

We also find these four figures – the bull, lion, eagle and man – depicted on the Royal Arch banners, as they are referenced in the associated degree ceremony where they are attributed to the Judaic Tribes of Ephraim, Judah, Dan and Reuben. The Four Living Creatures, or *Tetramorph*, as to which they are sometimes referred, are flanked by two *androsphinxes* who are themselves emblematic of the solstices, or Saints John, in the astrological interpretation of the standard. It is also notable that, within the precessional arrangement in keeping with the Taurian Age, the sign of Leo is inhabiting the *Keystone* position of the *Royal Arch* of the Heavens, representing the summer solstice's occurrence in the house of Leo, when the Sun is at its greatest strength, "[…] the beauty and glory of the day". A similar, though precessionally more current, rendition of this can be found on several 19th and 20th century Royal Arch tracing boards, where the cardinal sign of Cancer is represented as inhabiting the Keystone of the Arch.

34   Case, *Occult Fundamentals and Spiritual Unfoldment: Early Writings Vol. 1*, Fraternity of the Hidden Light, 2008, pp. 52-57.
35   *The Holy Bible* KJV, Ezekiel 1:10.
36   Ibid., Revelation 4:6-8.

This is, of course, referential to our current calendrical system in which the summer solstice occurs in the house of Cancer. In modern cartography, this astronomical event is described by the Tropic of Cancer.

Royal Arch Tracing Board – Summer Solstice in Cancer, the Pleiades, the Blazing Star (likely Sirius A/B) and the Fixed Signs of the Zodiac on the Heraldic Shield

To reiterate, it is of extreme Masonic significance, particularly as it pertains to the subject at hand, that this *Tetramorphic* alignment – viz. Taurus, Leo, Scorpio and Aquarius hosting the equinoxes and solstices – would have had its beginning in approximately the year 4000 BCE[37], which is, of course, the Masonic *Anno Lucis* and the commencement of the Taurian Age.

> *The cherub, or symbolic bull, which Moses placed at the gate of the Edenic world, bearing a fiery sword, is a sphinx, having a bull's body and a human head; it is the antique Assyrian sphinx, and the combat and victory of Mithras were its hieroglyphic analysis.*[38]

The Beginning of Freemasonry: Zodiac of 4000BC – Higgins, *Hermetic Masonry*, Kessinger, 2012, frontispiece

---

37   Carter, *An Introduction to Political Astrology (Mundane Astrology)*, Camelot Press, 1973, p. 74.
38   Levi, *Transcendental Magic: Its Doctrine and Ritual*, Martino Publishing, 2011, pp. 81-82.

THE PILLARS OF KING SOLOMON'S TEMPLE

The two Brazen Pillars of the Blue Lodge – one surmounted with the terrestrial globe, the other with the celestial – are said to be representations of those on the porch of King Solomon's Temple.[39] They have an immediate precedent in the obelisks of Dynastic Egypt in that they flank the portal and do not support the roof. The presence of pillars or obelisks, as a part of the architectural scheme of temples and other sacred structures, may be a symbolic allusion to the method by which many ancient temple structures were conjectured to have been aligned and subsequently *squared*. There are methods by which the shadows of precisely two standing poles (raised perpendicularly by means of a plumb line to stand at a right angle to a level plane) may be used to determine the cardinal directions based both on diurnal sunlight and, more accurately, by the biannual occurrence of the solstices.[40] Here we are again reminded of the Saints John, personifications of the solstices, whom will be discussed in greater detail below.

> *As two parallel columns, they denote the zodiacal signs of Cancer and Capricorn, which were formerly placed in the chamber of initiation to represent birth and death – the extremes of physical life. They accordingly signify the summer and winter solstices, now known to Freemasons under the comparatively modern appellation of the two "Saint Johns" [sic].[41]*

THE LODGE ROOM AND THE OFFICERS THEREIN

As previously discussed, the Masonic Lodge room is often said to be a microcosmic model of the Universe. "The form of a Lodge should always be an oblong square, in length, between the east and the west; in breadth, between the north and the south; in height, from earth to heaven; and in depth, from the surface to the center."[42] Additionally, much of the 'floor work' of the Lodge officers, particularly the act of circumambulation, has been interpreted to be an imitation of the Sun's apparent travels along

---

39   *The Holy Bible* KJV, 1 Kings 7:13–22, 41–42.

40   Brown, *Stellar Theology and Masonic Astronomy*, Merchant Books, 2008, pp. 79–82.

41   Hall, *The Secret Teachings of All Ages*, Dover, 2010 p. 262.

42   Sickels, *General Ahiman Rezon*, 1868, p. 76, sacred-texts.com, retrieved online.

the ecliptic.[43] The three principal officers of the Lodge – the Worshipful Master and the Senior and Junior Wardens – have their stations in the East, West and South, respectively. In Masonic ritual, these stations are said correspond to the diurnal events of sunrise, midday and sunset. These same diurnal attributions have been made to the Hindu *Trimurti* and to the trinary division of Egyptian solar personifications.[44]

> *It is very difficult to trace the origins of the Hindu triad. The idea of a triad of gods is rooted in the earliest Indian beliefs, perhaps the solar cults. The Sun possessed three qualities: warmth, light and burning rays. This appears to have contributed to the three essential functions with regard to the world process. Creation is thought to take place with the fertilizing warmth, preservation with the bright light, and destruction with the burning rays of the Sun.[45]*

> *Mention should also be made of the obvious solar and lunar representations on the Senior and Junior Deacon's rods and jewels. Reference to these luminaries is also made in Masonic Ritual, as to their situation in the Three Lesser Lights of the Lodge. Further, the Sun and Moon are ubiquitously present in tracing boards, aprons and other forms of regalia from all eras or Freemasonry.*

THE TEMPLUM, AUGURY AND THE OBLONG SQUARE

The Latin *templum* is the etymological root of the English word temple. The original usage of the word[46] was specifically in reference to the space designated for augury, an ancient form of divination based on the observation of the skies (*ex caelo*) and of birds (*ex avibus*) within a predetermined area and the interpretation of their positions and behaviors therein.[47] The *templum* was usually expressed as a double, or oblong square, i.e. a rectangle with two opposing sides that are exactly twice as long as

---

43   Mackey, *The Symbolism of Freemasonry*, Forgotten Books, 2012, p. 142.

44   Hall, *The Secret Teachings of All Ages*, Dover, 2010, pp. 93-95.

45   Dhavamony, *Hindu-Christian Dialogue: Theological Soundings and Perspectives*, Brill Rodopi, 2002.

46   Smith, *Dictionary of Greek and Roman Antiquities*, John Murray, 1875, pp. 174-179, retrieved online.

47   Ibid.

the two remaining sides. In this sense, the *templum* may be described more accurately as a rectangular vacancy than as an object, since it was less a thing-in-itself than a set of parameters delineating a *temple* in the night sky. Once again, we find that the terrestrial temple is actually a hermetic representation of its celestial counterpart.

> *The ordinary manner of taking the auspices, properly so called (i.e. ex caelo and ex avibus), was as follows: The person who was to take them first marked out with a wand (lituus) a division in the heavens called templum or tescum, within which he intended to make his observations. The station where he was to take the auspices was also separated by a solemn formula from the rest of the land, and was likewise called templum or tescum. He then proceeded to pitch a tent in it (tabernaculum capere), and this tent again was also called templum, or, more accurately, templum minus.*[48]

THE MOSAIC PAVEMENT AND THE BLAZING STAR

It has been suggested that mosaic patterns and tilework on the floor of ancient temples, from which the Checkered Pavement found in many Masonic Lodge rooms is descended, functioned not solely as aesthetic choices but also served as elaborate sundials.[49] Ancient architects utilized the effects of sunlight in their designs not only to position the edifice in space but also to accentuate its symbolic import. The trajectory of sunlight was directed through the portals of a building at specified angles depending on the time of year, based on various astronomical cycles, thus illuminating a certain area within the temple and thereby marking temporally significant events such as the equinoxes and solstices. This could be an elaboration on the same premise by which a temple is *squared* – by the utilization of two pillars marking the solstices, as discussed above. A properly oriented temple would thereby serve as a sort of annual, or seasonal, chronometer. This architecturally deliberate phenomenon can be observed in many structures around the globe.[50]

The Blazing Star, a five-pointed star usually within a circle, is often depicted in the center of the Checkered Pavement. This symbol is alter-

48   Ibid.
49   Brown, *Stellar Theology and Masonic Astronomy*, Merchant Books, 2008, p. 82.
50   Hiebert, *Celestial and Mathematical Precision in Ancient Architecture*, University of Manitoba, World-Mysteries.com, retrieved online.

nately said to represent the Sun, Sirius and Venus.[51] The Solar interpretation is obvious, in terms of the Sun's Masonic significance as being the "glory and beauty of the day", et cetera, but the theory of the Blazing Star as a representation of either Venus or Sirius provides us with much more substance for our contemplation.

The Blazing Star's relationship to Venus (also anciently known as the Morning and/or Evening Star) may best be illustrated by the fact that it is represented in the form of a pentagram. This significance comes primarily from the fact that Venus traces a five-petalled rosette at the completion of its synodic period, which is 583.9211 days – the amount of time it takes for the planet to return its originally observed position, relative to that of the Sun, as seen from the perspective of Earth – thus itself alluding to the pentagram. The pentagram, perhaps due to its association with either Pythagoreanism or as an elemental symbol in alchemy, is relatively common as a Masonic symbol and appears in the appendant body, the Order of the Eastern Star, as well as the Blazing Star.

> *The Star which guided them is that same Blazing Star, the image whereof we find in all initiations. To the Alchemists it is the sign of the Quintessence; to the Magists, the Grand Arcanum; to the Kabalists, the Sacred Pentagram. The study of this Pentagram could not but lead the Magi to the knowledge of the New Name which was about to raise itself above all names and cause all creatures capable of adoration to bend the knee.*[52]

The 'New Name' to which Pike refers is almost certainly that of Jesus (*Yahoshuah, Yeshua, Iesous,* IESV). This was Athanasius Kircher's *Pentagrammaton,* which is formed by adding the Hebrew letter *Shin* to the *Tetragrammaton* (YHVH + Sh = YHShVH). From this perspective, the Blazing Star may be associated with Jesus. In Revelation 22:16, Jesus states, "I, Jesus, have sent mine angel to testify unto you these things in the churches. I am the root and the offspring of David, *and the bright and morning star.*" From the Earth's vantage point, Venus may appear as much as 47 degrees away from the Sun. At these times, the planet may be seen just before sunrise as the *Morning Star* – Jesus – and just after sunset as the *Evening Star.* The pentagram which lead the magi and to which Pike refers in this passage is almost certainly Venus.

---

51   Brown, *Stellar Theology and Masonic Astronomy*, Merchant Books, 2008, p. 59.
52   Pike, *Morals and Dogma*, L. H. Jenkins Inc., 1947, p. 842.

The rosette created by Venus' synodic orbit, from the perspective of the Earth

A POINT WITHIN A CIRCLE

While there is no definitive interpretation of the Point Within a Circle diagram, a myriad of theories abound in the literature of Freemasonry. This diagram consists of a point at the center of a circle, bordered by two parallel, vertical lines – one representing Saint John the Baptist, and the other, Saint John the Evangelist – oftentimes distinguished with the letters *B* and *E*, respectively, and the Volume of Sacred Law at its top. The astronomical interpretation of this symbol posits that the circle with the point at its center is a solar glyph, as one would suspect, and that the two vertical lines are the tropics of Cancer and Capricorn, which mark the solstitial points.[53] Albert Pike argued against this interpretation on the basis that the parallel lines are vertical, not horizontal as one would expect them to be rendered in keeping with the common North-centric view of modern cartography.[54] However, if one considers that the East was the prominent directional orientation (consider the word: *orient*-ation – whose very root betrays this notion) of the ancient world, then the Point Within a Circle diagram would actually be a reasonably faithful representation of the solstitial phenomenon, with the V.S.L. representing the Light of dawn in the East.

[The Point Within A Circle, embordered by the Holy Saints John]

53   Mackey, *The Symbolism of Freemasonry*, Forgotten Books, 2012, p. 115.
54   Pike, *Morals and Dogma*, L. H. Jenkins Inc., 1947, p. 17.

THE WORKING TOOLS

In speculative Freemasonry, the working tools of the operative Craft are utilized symbolically to inculcate certain moral and ethical lessons. Operatively, these tools are used to realize geometrical abstractions in three-dimensional space and have been essential to architecture and construction for millennia. Notably, these tools have analogous, spatial counterparts in both navigation and astronomy. Cartesian coordinates (x, y and z) can be discerned in all the sciences dependent upon geometry and, because of this fact, the instruments used share similar applicability concerning spatial relations and coordinates such as up-and-down (the plumb), left-and-right (the level) and forward-and-backward (the square). Bearing this relationship in mind, the analogous relationship between the plumb, square and level of Freemasonry and the astrolabe, T-crossbar and quadrant of ancient astronomy becomes clear. Though the subjects of their measurement and observation differ, the technical applicability of these instruments are identical. It is important for us to bear in mind the connection between the Working Tools of the operative Mason and the instruments of the ancient astronomer if we wish to appreciate the ancient and common origins of these arts. As we consider these relationships, we are again reminded of the deliberately sequential nature of the *Quadrivium*, which consists of (in order): *arithmetic* (pure number), *geometry* (number in fixed space), *music* (number in time) and *astronomy* (number in space-time).

THE LEGEND OF THE THIRD DEGREE

Before we begin to apply the astro-mythological interpretation to Freemasonry's central allegory, we must first recount the narrative in the form it is given in the Masonic Lodge. The Legend of the Third Degree, also known as the Hiramic Legend, is the most prominent initiatory ritual in Freemasonry and constitutes the culmination of the Third Degree ceremony, which is the rite of the Master Mason. The Legend utilizes the personas and setting from the Old Testament narrative of the building of King Solomon's Temple in a ritual-drama designed to inculcate moral and ethical sentiments such as personal integrity and fraternal loyalty. However, as with any allegory, there are various alternate inroads of interpretation available to us. Depending upon which interpretive keys we apply, we may discover a variety of themes that have been hidden – some perhaps unconsciously deposited by the author or authors, as is the case in many tales coming to us from world mythology, and some occulted by design. The following is a brief synopsis of the narrative as it exists in its currently practiced form.[55]

The narrative takes place in and around King Solomon's Temple, near its completion. According to the legend, it was the custom of the Temple's chief architect, Grand Master Hiram Abiff, the son of a widow from the Naphtali tribe of Israel, to retire to the *Sanctum Sanctorum* of the Temple at noon to offer adorations to God and draw designs for the workmen on his trestleboard. Unbeknownst to him, three Fellowcrafts had entered into a plot to extort the secrets of a Master Mason from Hiram Abiff in order that they might receive Master's wages and be free to travel.

At one hour past noon, Hiram Abiff attempted to pass out of the South gate of the Temple where he was accosted by Jubela, one of the three Fellowcraft, who demanded the secrets. Hiram Abiff thrice refused the request and was consequently struck with a twenty-four inch gauge across the throat. He then attempted to leave the Temple by the West gate where he was accosted by Jubelo, who also thrice demanded the secrets and was refused, striking Hiram Abiff across the chest with a Mason's square. Mortally wounded, Hiram Abiff then attempted to pass out of the East gate where he met with Jubelum, who thrice demanded the secrets, was refused, and struck the Grand Master in the head with a setting maul, killing him on the spot. The Three Ruffians, as they are henceforth known, bury the body in the rubbish of the Temple and agree to reconvene at the site at midnight.

That evening, they carry the body on a Westerly course to the brow of a hill where they proceed to bury the remains of Hiram Abiff in a grave dug six feet East to West, six feet North to South and six feet deep. As a marker, should they need to return to the site, they place a sprig of Acacia at the head of the grave. They devise a plan to escape via the seaport Joppa but they are refused by a sea captain who asks them to provide King Solomon's seal that they might travel.

Meanwhile, there is confusion among the workman at the Temple. It is unusual that there would be no designs upon the trestleboard and all apartments are searched for the Grand Master Hiram Abiff. A role is called amongst the Fellowcrafts and it is found that Jubela, Jubelo and Jubelum are missing. Twelve Fellowcrafts come forward, clad in aprons and gloves, imploring pardon. They, along with the Three Ruffians, had

---

55   *Official Masonic Ritual*, Grand Lodge of Connecticut, 2010, pp. 221-252.

been involved in the plot to extort the secrets of a Master Mason but they abandoned the plan before it was enacted. They say that they fear that the others may have proceeded with their devious design. The Twelve Fellowcrafts are commanded to search in four parties of three to each of the cardinal directions for the three ruffians and bring them to justice. They are told that, if they are unsuccessful, they shall be put to death.

While on their search, the Fellowcrafts that had traveled on a Westerly course come into contact with a wayfaring man near the port at Joppa who informs them that he had seen three workers from the Temple seeking passage out of the country. The Fellowcrafts agree divide and gather intelligence to bring back to the King. One of the Fellowcrafts decides to rest and contemplate his predicament on the brow of a hill before turning back. He grabs hold of a sprig of Acacia to assist his rising and finds it very suspicious that it should have given away so easily from the soil. He calls for his companions and, while relaying this singular occurrence to them, they hear the voices of the three ruffians emitting from a nearby cave. Jubela, Jubelo and Jubelum are seized, brought to King Solomon, sentenced to death and executed.

Commanded by King Solomon, the Fellowcrafts then repair to the brow of the hill where the body was discovered in search of the Master's Word, of which Hiram Abiff had the needed third part, without which the Word would be lost. The body, having been interred for fifteen days, had decomposed somewhat and a key to, or sign of the Word is not present but the Grand Master's jewel is found and brought back to King Solomon. King Solomon and Hiram King of Tyre, the Grand Master, second-in-command at the building of the Temple, lead a procession to the grave where they intend to raise the body in order that the Grand Master Hiram Abiff's remains may be decently deposited in a grave within the Temple's *Sanctum Sanctorum*. However, due to the decomposition, when trying to raise the Grand Master's body from the grave by using the Apprentice's grip, the skin slipped from the flesh. Hiram King of Tyre then attempted to raise the body by applying the grip of a Fellocraft but the flesh cleaved from the bone. King Solomon, after some reflection and contemplation, decided to apply the strong grip of a Master Mason, or Lion's Paw, upon which the body was raised.

The initiate is told the moral and ethical interpretation of the Hiramic Legend and is admonished to "imitate Grand Master Hiram Abiff in his virtuous conduct, his unfeigned piety to his God and his inflexible fidelity to his trust." Upon conferral of this degree, one is generally struck by the fact that this is a strange and somewhat morbid ritual of obvious antiquity

– particularly if one is familiar with the general structure of initiatory rites of passage, especially those of a chthonic nature. Surely, there are much easier and less convoluted ways to teach personal integrity – as if that were, indeed, posited to be the total interpretive sum. However, when one begins to apply the various keys of interpretation, one may begin to discern the emergence of other, less conspicuous facets of this legend. As with many other finely constructed allegories, one finds that the application of each interpretive lens yields yet another dimension of the narrative and with it, a fresh insight. We will now apply the solar and astrological interpretive keys to this central-most Legend in Freemasonry.

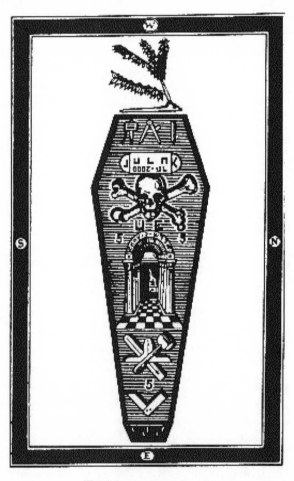

Third degree tracing board

AN INTERPRETATION OF THE HIRAMIC LEGEND
AS A SOLAR ALLEGORY

When we consider the narrative arc of the Hiramic Legend, vis-à-vis the Sun's apparent passage through the twelve houses of the zodiac as seen from the perspective of the Earth, the solar and astrological nature of this allegory begins to emerge. This is accomplished, in this case, by means of drawing a hermetic parallel between microcosm and macrocosm.

In order to apply the astrological interpretive key to the Hiramic Legend, we must first begin by temporally orienting ourselves to the *Anno Lucis*, viz. 4000 BCE. At this astrological alignment, we will find the equinoxes and solstices inhabited by the fixed signs of the zodiac: Taurus, Leo, Scorpio and Aquarius, sequentially, beginning with Taurus at the vernal equinox, i.e. the Taurian Age. From the vantage point of this Taurian precessional configuration, we will observe the summer solstice (June 20th or 21st) as occurring in Leo. It is Masonically notable, of course, that the Feast of Saint John the Baptist, itself a solstitial celebration, also occurs in this vicinity (June 24th). Here we find the Sun at its highest point in the heavens – "the glory and beauty of the day", or the Keystone of the Royal Arch. It is in this position, 'High Twelve' in the *Sanctum Sanctorum* of the Temple, that the allegory of the Hiramic Legend begins and, after one complete annual revolution, ends.

As the Sun passes from the House of Leo into that of Virgo, we make note of the fact that Virgo is attributed to the Tribe of *Naphtali* in the *Mazzaroth* of Job.[56] Also notable is the sheaf of wheat in the House of Virgo, which is carried by the virgin in most personifications of this constellation, particularly as it pertains to the name of the pass grip of a Fellowcraft Mason and also its significance in what has come to us from the Eleusinian Mysteries, wherein initiates were said to have experienced "an ear of corn in silence reaped."[57] In the Masonic allegory, Hiram Abiff is referred to as being a widow's son. Similarly, the Egyptian solar personification Horus was also the son of a widow, as his father Osiris' death at the hands of Set left Isis widowed.[58] Notably, Isis was also anciently associated with the constellation Virgo.[59]

The story of the Hiramic legend closely follows the apparent path of the Sun along the ecliptic and through the houses of the zodiac, especially in its mythological connection with the symbolic death of the Sun (in au-

---

56   Mathers, *Twelve Signs and Twelve Tribes*, Aquarian, 1983, retrieved online.
57   Nilsson, *Greek Popular Religion*, Bibliolife, 2009, p. 61.
58   Bulfinch, *Bulfinch's Mythology*, Barnes & Noble, 2006, pp. 271-272.
59   Hall, *The Secret Teachings of All Ages*, Dover, 2010, p. 552.

tumn/winter) and its subsequent resurrection (spring). As the Sun reaches the autumnal equinox, it is accosted by Scorpio, the scorpion – betrayer and backbiter – who deals the first blow to the Sun's strength. In the Legend, this blow is dealt with the twenty-four inch gauge, which has solar significance in that there are twenty-four hours in one diurnal rotation. Sagittarius and Capricorn, follow in succession. This is analogous to the first blows that Hiram suffered as he attempted to flee the Temple. Note that, in the narrative, the third and final blow to the Grandmaster is dealt with a setting maul. Seeing as Jupiter is the planetary ruler of Sagittarius and that hammer-wielding *Thor* is the correspondingly Jupiterian deity in the Norse pantheon[60], the significance of which is due to the use of a setting maul in the allegory. At this point, the Sun is left effectively *dead* in the "rubbish of the Temple", i.e. the disintegrating vegetation and seasonal detritus left over from the previous summer and autumnal harvest. The three autumnal months reach the completion of their portion of the annual cycle at the winter solstice, which is represented in the allegory by 'Low Twelve'.

At this point in the astrological cycle, the Sun, which always appears to travel on a Westerly course in its diurnal cycle, is then figuratively interred in a grave, and in the Hiramic legend, the body of Hiram is then interred in a grave which is six feet east and west, six feet north and south, and six feet deep (in the Ritual of several states).[61] Due to the specificity of the dimensions of the grave in the allegory, it is probable that they carry symbolic import. One interpretation is that they may be an allusion to materiality. This 6'X6'X6' cube is an apt symbol for materiality for three reasons: first, that a cube unfolded is a cross, and both the cube and the cross are commonly associated with the idea of materiality; second, that a carbon atom, the material basis of all living things, consists of six protons, six neutrons and six electrons; and, third, that Revelation 13:18 in the King James Version of *The Holy Bible* refers to 666 as a human number, the number of a man. The body of Hiram Abiff is interred here for fifteen days, which may share the same symbolic import as the fifteen pieces of Osiris' dismembered body for which Isis searched in the Egyptian agricultural Mystery.[62] Both are likely allusions to the 14.25 days of waning Moon, as it appears to lose pieces of itself during one half of the lunar phase cycle, which totals 29.5 days.

In the Legend, a sprig of Acacia is placed at the site of this temporary

60   Online Etymology Dictionary, *Thursday*, etymonline.com, retrieved online.
61   *Official Masonic Ritual*, Grand Lodge of Connecticut, 2010, p. 229.
62   Bulfinch, *Bulfinch's Mythology*, Barnes & Noble, 2006, pp. 271-272.

interment. This may allude to the hope of regeneration, realized by the vernal equinox and coinciding with the emergence of foliage associated with springtime, and to the subsequent extrapolation of that symbolic concept as it pertains to the immortality of the human soul (Also see: Newman, *Alchemically Stoned*, The Laudable Pursuit, 2017; a brilliantly developed thesis on the possible entheobotanical import of this powerful Masonic symbol). In this sense, the sprig of Acacia shares much of the same symbolic content with that of the Christmas tree; itself perhaps the most universally recognized symbolic representation of the winter solstice. It is also worthy of note that the Feast of Saint John the Evangelist occurs on December 27th, comfortably within the vicinity of the winter solstice, and other holidays marking this event, such as *Saturnalia*, Yuletide and Christmas.

The Three Ruffians, themselves representatives of the autumnal months, then try to escape, also by a westerly course, when they are refused passage by a seafaring man at the seaport, Joppa. This situation, in the astrological interpretation, represents a symbolic dramatization of the Sun's passage through the house of Pisces in mid-winter.

Meanwhile, there is confusion in the Temple, all the various apartments are searched, again analogous to Isis' search for the pieces of Osiris, and the Three Ruffians are noted to be missing. The last letters of their names, Jubel-*A*, Jubel-*O* and Jubel-*UM*, form a word sufficiently close to the Hindu *AUM*, or *OM*, to merit investigation. The word *AUM* has also been linked to the *Trimurti* – Brahma, Vishnu and Shiva – who are also referred to as the creator, preserver and destroyer, and are together frequently recognized as a tripartite solar personification.[63]

> *The Hindu word AUM represented the three Powers combined in their Deity: Brahma, Vishnu, and Siva; or the Creating, Preserving, and Destroying Powers: A, the first; U or O-O, the second; and M, the third. This word could not be pronounced, except by the letters: for its pronunciation as one word was said to make Earth tremble, and even the Angels of Heaven to quake for fear.*[64]

The twelve Fellowcrafts who come forward to confess their parts in the conspiracy and are subsequently dispatched in four parties of three to the cardinal directions. Astrologically, these twelve represent either the twelve calendar months or the twelve houses of the zodiac, and are divided

---

63   Higgins, *AUM: The Lost Word*, Kessinger, 2012, p. 6.
64   Pike, *Morals and Dogma*, L. H. Jenkins Inc., 1947, p. 620.

into the astrological triplicities, which assign three zodiacal houses to each of the classical elements: fire (Aries, Leo and Sagittarius), air (Gemini, Libra and Aquarius), water (Cancer, Scorpio and Pisces) and earth (Taurus, Virgo and Capricorn).[65]

Three of the twelve Fellowcrafts, those representing the winter months, take a westerly course where they meet a *wayfaring man*; the personified Aquarian, next in zodiacal succession after the *seafaring man*, Pisces. The Fellowcrafts are also said to be clad in gloves and aprons. This may also be interpreted to be an allusion to the winter passage from Capricorn (winter solstice) to Aries (vernal equinox), since gloves were frequently made from goatskin, hence the term *kid gloves*, and that the apron is made from lambskin; lambs being immature rams. They come upon the 'brow of a hill' where one of the Fellowcrafts makes note of the sprig of Acacia transplanted by the Ruffians – both the brow of the hill and the sprig of Acacia symbolize the vernal equinox and the emergence of spring. They hear the voices of the Three Ruffians emitting from a nearby cave. It should here be noted that the cave is a frequent feature of the vernal stage of many solar allegories, such as those of *Krishna*, Mithras and Jesus Christ, wherein Jesus is temporarily interred in a cave – after being crucified on the brow of the hill, *Golgotha*, of course – and rises from the dead at Easter, itself a vernal celebration.[66]

That there are Three Ruffians and Three Fellowcrafts corresponding to the autumnal and winter quarters, respectively, is especially significant because the seasons each account for the 'fourth part of a circle', which is a square. Similarly, the three vernal months correspond to the grips used to *raise* the Sun. The grip of the Entered Apprentice is symbolized by Gemini, the twins, represented by the two Brazen Pillars on the porch of King Solomon's Temple. The grip of the Fellowcraft is represented by Cancer, the crab, whose 'winding' or zig-zag style of walking gains significance when considered in regard to figurative location of the lecture accompanying this Degree: the Winding Staircase. Next, of course, is the grip of Master Mason, which is fittingly represented by Leo the Lion, the house in which the summer solstice occurs at the *Anno Lucis* in the Taurian precessional age. Using the Royal Arch banner as a key, we also find that the Lion is associated with the Tribe of Judah, as is mentioned in the ritual. And thus the Sun is *raised* from a "dead level to a living perpendicular" and reconducted to its former position in the Royal Arch of the Heavens, the *Sanctum Sanctorum* at High Twelve, i.e. the summer solstice.

---

65   Case, *Occult Fundamentals and Spiritual Unfoldment: Early Writings Vol. 1*, Fraternity of the Hidden Light, 2008, pp. 52-57.
66   Bede, *The Reckoning of Time*, 725 CE, retrieved online.

CONCLUSION OF SECTION II

In summary, it is hoped that the assertions made in the foregoing have illuminated the prevalence and significance of both the conspicuous and inconspicuous solar and astrological allusions occurring in Freemasonry's diagrammatic content, banners, standards, insignia, regalia, Lodge room, and in several aspects of the Fraternity's ritual and initiatory degree work. Additionally, it has been illustrated that Freemasonry, having served as a repository for a wealth of symbolic and allegorical material of a generally astrological nature, has perpetuated elements common to many ancient Mystery traditions.

SECTION III:

ELEMENTS OF CLASSICAL MYTHOLOGY IN MODERN FREEMASONRY

ELEMENTS OF CLASSICAL MYTHOLOGY IN MODERN FREEMASONRY

"Within the characters and events portrayed in a mythological account, one finds moral lessons, the nature and relationship between deities and man, virtues, vices, and values – all areas of concern in Masonry. [...] ancient myth often finds its expression in Masonic symbolism."[1]

For millennia, references to specific aspects of world mythology and folklore have served to provide a foundation whereupon newer ritualistic, dramatic and literary structures have been erected. Classical Mythology, particularly that of the Greeks and Romans, has provided a valuable subtext through inference and allusion, if not blatant appropriation, for many subsequent narratives. To attribute grey eyes to a character in a modern novel, for instance, is to evoke an Athenian element, perhaps alluding to the possession of keen reasoning powers or a propensity for strategic thought – all aspects of the ancient Homeric depiction of "grey-eyed Athena". In the vernacular of literary criticism, this device is called intertextuality which, in applications such as the example above, functions as an economical method of utilizing short allusions to familiar themes as a means to add contextual depth to the subject at hand without having to unpack the root narrative in its entirety.

Thanks largely to Thomas Bulfinch's and Edith Hamilton's *Mythologies*, stories of the Titans, Olympians and, Heroes of the Classical Era have been introduced into modern popular culture as a source of influence. Even if we don't know of them first hand, through direct exposure via the epics and tragedies, etc., we are aware of their personas from a near-constant referential barrage – everything from the names of the planets and the days of the week, to all ages of painting, sculpture, literature, and architecture bear the unmistakable stamp of Classical Mythology. We know what someone means when they say that one has the *Midas* touch, or an *Oedipus* complex; commonplace words such as *fury, echo* and *panic,* each have its origin

1   Rex Hutchens, *Pillars of Wisdom,* The Supreme Council A.A.S.R., 1995, p. 61.

in a mythological persona, and have been completely assimilated into our everyday language. The influence of Classical Mythology is socially and culturally inescapable in the Western World.

When one examines Masonic ritual and symbolism through the interpretive lens of Classical Mythology, the correspondences immediately begin to present themselves and become, at times, strikingly obvious. These inferences and allusions are present in the officer's jewels, the Furniture of the Lodge Room, the Deacon's rods, even in the rituals themselves, to such an extent that almost everywhere one cares to look can be found some vestige of the great mythological systems of the world.

It is the purpose of this Section of the current work to enumerate some of these mythologically significant parallels and to illustrate that Freemasonry not only constitutes a living mythological system, replete with its own syncretized body of archetypes and lore, but also that the function of Masonic ritual and initiation serves an identical purpose to that of myth in other sociocultural systems. Considering that the further comparison and exploration of our subject is dependent on an understanding of what we mean by the function of both Freemasonry and mythology, we will attempt to clarify the relevant aspects of these points in their turn.

Prosopon - Greek theater masks, originally used in Dionysian Mysteries and satyr plays

THE FUNCTIONS OF MYTH

The common consensus among most modern anthropologists is that the origins of the gods may be found in the personified forces of nature; Zeus – the thunderous sky-god, Poseidon – the god of the raging seas, Hades – the chthonic deity at the center of the Earth, along with various agricultural and fertility deities, dutifully placated by their respective cults, were personifications of natural objects and phenomena.[2] This animistic approach thereby afforded man an opportunity to form a relationship with his environment that could be influenced by ritualism and the practice of what Frazer had termed 'sympathetic magic'.

> *Both branches of magic, the homeopathic and the contagious, may conveniently be comprehended under the general name of Sympathetic Magic, since both assume that things act on each other at a distance through a secret sympathy, the impulse being transmitted from one to the other by means of what we may conceive as a kind of invisible ether, not unlike that which is postulated by modern science for a precisely similar purpose, namely, to explain how things can physically affect each other through space which appears to be empty.[3]*

Conversely, according to the works of psychologist C.G. Jung, the various pantheons, be they that of the Hindu, Egyptian, Greco-Roman, et cetera, were personified symbolic sets of archetypal forces within the collective psyche of man. According to Jung, the gods and heroes are rendered in the psyche as compartmentalized aspects of the Self, engaged in a constant melee of dissonance and resolution.[4]

> *[...] the images of the great myths and religions still have about them a little of the "cloudy" nature of absolute knowledge in that they always seem to contain more than we can assimilate consciously, even by means of elaborate interpretations. They always retain an ineffable and mysterious quality that seems to reveal to us more than we can really know.[5]*

---

2   *Encyclopedia of Religion and Nature*, Continuum, 2005, p. 78.
3   Frazer, *The Golden Bough*, Oxford, 2009, p. 27.
4   Jung, *Collected Works*, Vol. 3, Bollingen, 1968, par. 549.
5   Von Franz, *Psyche and Matter*, Shambhala, 1988, unpaginated PDF, retrieved online

Expressing an anthropologically complimentary sentiment, the mythologist Joseph Campbell wrote: "Dream is the personalized myth, myth the depersonalized dream; both myth and dream are symbolic in the same general way of the dynamic of the psyche. But in the dream the forms are quirked by the peculiar troubles of the dreamer, whereas in myth the problems and solutions sown are directly valid for all mankind,"[6] thereby referring to the body of world myth and folklore as the collective dream of mankind. These psychoanalytical approaches to mythology seek to employ archetypal identities as placeholders for groups of concepts, both abstract and concrete, in an effort to catalog and eventually integrate these seemingly disparate aspects of the Self into a unified whole.

Prosopon – theater mask

6   Campbell, *The Hero with a Thousand Faces*, Bollingen, 1973, p. 19.

THE INITIATORY FUNCTION OF FREEMASONRY

There are many interpretive keys whose application may yield a greater understanding and promote a synthesis of the material inherent in Masonic ritual and symbolism. When one takes an interpretive approach to the rites of Freemasonry similar to those employed by Campbell, Jung and Frazer in their attempts to unravel the great mythological and Mystery systems of the world, many parallels begin to emerge and one begins to see that some very common mythological motifs have provided a mysterious source of buoyancy to Freemasonry. Furthermore, bearing in mind that both the general body of world mythology and the myriad of initiatory tributaries to modern Masonry disappear in the mists of time, it is all but impossible to say at which developmental stage the comingling of these concepts occurred.

Like all initiatory rites, those of Freemasonry are designed to bring the initiate from their previous station in life into a new one, hence the usage of the term *initiate* – to cause something to begin.[7] When the transformational element occurs, the initiate finds himself irretrievably catapulted into a new paradigm in his consciousness. This is most commonly accomplished by means of an allegorical ritual-drama consisting of some form of ordeal. The use of an allegorical ritual-drama as the central component in the initiatory process is common to nearly all of the Ancient Mysteries of which we are aware.[8] Significantly, this device is also employed in Freemasonry's Blue Lodge and several of its appendant bodies.

MYTHOLOGICAL MOTIFS IN FREEMASONRY

As was previously stated, it is the purpose of this Section to enumerate some of the examples of mythological motifs present in Freemasonry. The following will be limited to a few of the more glaring examples but the reader is encouraged to extrapolate this information and to apply this interpretive lens to their studies and research on their chosen initiatory path within the Western Esoteric Tradition.

---

7 Merriam Webster Dictionary, retrieved online.
8 Vail, *The Ancient Mysteries and Modern Masonry*, Forgotten Books, 2012, pp. 38-60.

THE ORDERS OF ARCHITECTURE

The Orders of Architecture, as described in Vitruvius' *De Architectura*[9], are discussed in the Masonic Fellowcraft Degree lecture. Visual representations of these orders are also commonly found in the Lodge room, either in two- or three-dimensional form. Significantly, each of the three ancient Greek architectural orders, the Doric, Ionic and Corinthian, are associated with one of the Three Principal Supports of the Masonic Lodge, which are Wisdom, Strength and Beauty.[10]

The Doric order is said to denote strength and was held sacred to Ares, the god of war. In ancient building practices, the Doric order was used in the construction of structures which served a martial purpose, such as those devoted to warfare or defense.[11] This style is especially notable for its relative simplicity. It is the least ornamental of the original Greek orders of architecture, thereby evoking a martial atmosphere through its clean, unembellished lines. In Freemasonry, the Doric column is associated with Strength – the Senior Warden's station.

The Ionic order of architecture denotes wisdom and was held sacred to Athena. Being between the Doric and Corinthian in overall complexity, it is moderate and tempered in appearance. This style was most frequently employed in houses of learning, such as academies and libraries.[12] In the Masonic Lodge, the Ionic column is attributed to Principal Support of Wisdom, which is further associated with the Worshipful Master's station.

The Corinthian order of architecture was employed when a structure was to be designated for an artistic or aesthetic purpose, such as a museum. This order was considered sacred to Aphrodite, the goddess of beauty. The Corinthian style was the most ornate of the three original, ancient Greek orders of architecture.[13] In Freemasonry, this Corinthian column is fittingly associated with Beauty and the office of Junior Warden. This style is ornamented with acanthus leaves, which were used in funerary celebrations in the ancient Mediterranean. Consequently, the acanthus has come to symbolize the immortality of the human soul, which gains Masonic significance when we note that this order of column is situated in the South, the station of Grand Master Hiram Abiff. The acanthus is also notable

9   Vitruvius, *De Architectura*, Penguin, 2009, Book IV, Chapter 1.
10   Brown, *Stellar Theology and Masonic Astronomy*, Merchant Books, 2008, p. 101.
11   Vitruvius, *De Architectura*, Penguin, 2009, Book IV, Chapter 3.
12   Ibid., Book III, Chapter 5.
13   Ibid., Book IV, Chapter 1.

when we compare it to the similar symbolism of the sprig of Acacia, which is associated with the grave of Hiram Abiff and thereby with immortality.

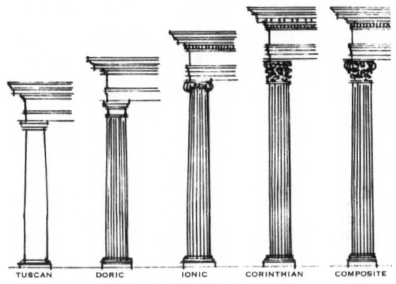

The Orders of Architecture

THE BRAZEN PILLARS

Representations of the Two Brazen Pillars that are said to have stood on the porch of King Solomon's Temple[14] are situated in the West of the Masonic Lodge room and are referenced in the lecture accompanying the Fellowcraft degree. The capital of each pillar is decorated with pomegranates, lilies and netting.[15] Pomegranates have figured prominently in various mythological cycles from the Mediterranean. Perhaps the most notable appearance is in the myth of Persephone's imperfect ascent from the Underworld wherein Hades had given her pomegranate seeds, thus obliging her to spend a part of the year in his kingdom. The lily is associated with the Olympian goddess, Hera, and are said to have sprouted from drops of milk that had spilled from her breast as she nursed Herakles. The Brazen Pillars have also been equated to the Pillars of Herakles[16], which will be discussed below.

---

14   *The Holy Bible* KJV, 1 Kings 7:13–22, 41–42.
15   Ibid., Jeremiah 52:21–22.
16   Higgins, *Hermetic Masonry*, Kessinger, 2012, p. 65.

THE PILLARS OF HERAKLES AND THE
MEDITERRANEAN MODEL OF THE LODGE ROOM

There is an interesting, though perhaps less-than-tenable, argument which posits that the basic layout of the Masonic Lodge room is a model of the Ancient World, particularly those areas that border the Mediterranean Sea.[17] It is notable that the Latin *mediterraneus*, the etymological predecessor of the word *Mediterranean*, means 'the middle of the Earth's surface'. According to this interpretation, the Two Brazen Pillars of the Lodge represent the Pillars of Herakles; and are called such because, in Classical Mythology, Herakles is said to have brought these pillars down. The Strait of Gibraltar, which connects the Atlantic Ocean to the Mediterranean Sea and divides the continents of Europe and Africa, has been conjectured to be the site of the Pillars of Herakles. Individually, the Pillars are represented by the Spain's Rock of Gibraltar to the North and Morocco's Jebel Musa to the South. Like those of the Masonic Lodge room, these Pillars are found at the 'West gate' of the Mediterranean. The candidate for initiation must pass through these two Pillars in order to gain entrance to the Masonic Temple, in imitation of one's passage through those which were situated on the Portico of King Solomon's Temple, flanking its entrance.

In this geographical Lodge room, the Grecian island of Crete inhabits the vicinity of the Masonic Altar. Crete was the site of the ancient Minoan civilization and King Minos' labyrinth, which was constructed by Daedalus to house the Minotaur, in Classical Mythology. The ubiquitous Taurian elements of Minoan civilization, and the attendant mythological corpus, are likely referential to the Taurian precessional age[18], which began in approximately 4000 BCE – in the vicinity of the Masonic *Anno Lucis*. Significantly, we also find both Tyre (in modern-day Lebanon), from whence both Grandmasters King Hiram and Hiram Abiff hailed, and Jerusalem in the East of the Mediterranean Lodge. Lastly, we find the Junior Warden's station in North Africa – this may be read as a connection between Hiram Abiff's death and its correlations to the Osirian mythological cycle, in which Osiris' body comes to be entwined within an Acacia tree at Byblos.

This geographical juxtaposition allows us to superimpose the template of mythological locales, events and narratives of the ancient Mediterranean – such as the quests of Odysseus, Jason and Theseus – onto the

---

17   Mackey, *The Symbolism of Freemasonry*, Forgotten Books, 2012, pp. 102-104.
18   Hancock, *Fingerprints of the Gods*, Three Rivers, 1995, pp. 238-241.

Lodge room, thereby gaining yet another intriguing vantage point from which to appreciate both Classical Mythology and Masonic ritual, furniture and symbolism.

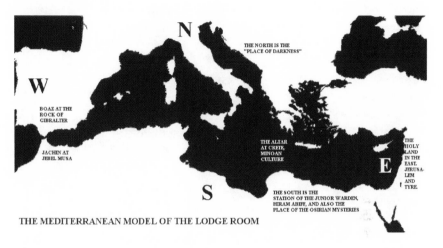

THE MEDITERRANEAN MODEL OF THE LODGE ROOM

MASONIC LODGE OFFICERS
AND MYTHOLOGICAL ARCHETYPES

There are many points of similarity between the attributes of mythological archetypes and the duties of Masonic Lodge Officers. We will elucidate but a few of these here, which will serve to establish a useful interpretive lens, which one may employ in order to independently extrapolate the presence of many other mythologically archetypal functions within the ritualism and officer roles of Freemasonry.

Two of the Senior Deacon's duties, as stated in the opening of a Lodge, is to receive and conduct candidates and to carry orders from the Worshipful Master in the East. These functions are reflections of the hermetic or mercurial mythological archetype. Hermes, who was syncretized with Mercury in the Roman Pantheon, was often depicted as the *psychopompos*: the conductor of the souls of the dead – and, in a few cases, the living – to and from the Underworld.[19] He brought Persephone back from Hades at the behest of Demeter; Hermes guided Orpheus to fetch Eurydice, he conducted Theseus, Psyche and Herakles on their brief sojourns into the underworld. Similarly, Herm-Anubis (due to Ptolemaic syncretization, particularly in Hellenic Alexandria, Hermes became fused with Anubis in

---

19   Campbell, *The Hero with a Thousand Faces*, Bollingen, 1973, p. 72.

this archetypal role) conducted the recently deceased to the Duat, which, in Egyptian Mythology, corresponds to Hades or Tartarus.[20] We see this soul guiding function throughout the various incarnations of Hermes depending on the mythological or religious tradition in which the archetype appears. Be it the Greek Hermes conducting the recently deceased to and from Hades, the Egypto-Hellenic Herm-Anubis conducting the same to their judgement in the Duat, or any of his other personifications, we find this to be a common function of the hermetic archetype.[21] This is mirrored in the responsibilities of the Senior Deacon of the Masonic Lodge whose duty is to "receive and conduct candidates". He is responsible for conducting the initiate during the circumambulation and also during the enactment of the Hiramic Legend. Additionally, the Senior Deacon communicates the password for the Brother initiate during the Fellowcraft and Master Mason Degrees, which is also a common hermetic function in myth and ritual.[22]

Herm-Anubis – chthonic *psychopompos*

20   Budge, *The Gods of the Egyptians*, vol. 2, Dover, 2013, pp. 263-266.
21   Bulfinch, *Bulfinch's Mythology*, Barnes & Noble, 2006, p. 271.
22   New Larousse *Encyclopedia of Mythology*, Hamlyn Publishing Group, 1972, p. 123.

An interesting astro-mythological explanation for this hermetic attribute may have something to do with the fact that the planet Mercury, whose orbit is in very close proximity to that of the Sun from the perspective of the Earth, appears to guide the Sun into the Underworld – night, in this analogy – at the close of every day. This is particularly significant when we consider the chthonic arc (i.e. 'Low Twelve') of a certain 'perilous journey' upon which the *mercurial* Senior Deacon conducts the *solar* candidate in Masonic ritual. The Senior Deacon also serves the mercurial function of messenger within the Masonic Lodge, carrying messages from the Worshipful Master in the East to the Senior Warden in the West and elsewhere about the Lodge – just as the wing-footed Mercury, the herald, carried messages to and from the Olympians.[23]

It is also notable that the Secretary of the Masonic Lodge is responsible for recording the minutes of the Lodge's communications; this was an attribute of Thoth, who was the scribe and hermetic archetype of the Egyptian *Neteru*.[24] Thoth was fused with Hermes in Hellenistic Egypt – notably, in the personage of Hermes Trismegistus (Thrice Great), to which Titus Flavius Clemens (Clement of Alexandria, an early Christian church father and convert from Pagandom) had attributed the forty-two books of the *Corpus Hermeticum*. Due to his being considered the personification of the archetypal scribe, Thoth-Hermes was thus often referred to as the 'writer of all books'.[25]

The Marshal is the Lodge's conductor and Director of Ceremonies. His principal role is to organize and conduct processions – a tradition that comes to us largely from the martial victory processions of the Homeric epics, such as that which occurred at the termination of the *Iliad*. This ancient tradition of processions, victory laps and parades also formed the conceptual basis of such disparate points as the carousel (or, merry-go-round), trump cards and the very word *triumph* – the latter stemming from the Italian *trionfi*.[26]

The foregoing examples, along with many other aspects of Freemasonry's initiatory degree work, substantiate the Craft's association with the hermetic arts and the mythological basis of Classical and Epic Literature. The presence of these attributes in Masonic ritual and symbolism also speak to the universality of these themes in initiatory rites and, perhaps most significantly, how these concepts, which have found expression in all cultures, may stem from the deepest regions of mankind's collective psyche.

---

23   Hamilton, *Mythology*, Grand Central, 2011, pp. 30-31.
24   Budge, *The Gods of the Egyptians*, vol. 1, Dover, 2013, p. 9.
25   Hall, *The Secret Teachings of All Ages*, Dover, 2010, pp. 54-56.
26   Nichols, *Jung and Tarot*, Weiser, 1984, pp. 3-5.

THE MYTHOLOGICAL IMPORT OF
THE OFFICER'S JEWELS

In Masonic regalia, the role of each officer is designated by a particular jewel which is either appended to a collar or fixed atop a rod. The Senior and Junior Stewards' rods are ornately capped with a cornucopia within a pinecone, both of which come to us direct from Classical Mythology. The cornucopia is considered to be the horn of Amalthea, the she-goat that suckled Zeus in his infancy. The cornucopia also appears as a symbol associated with the grain mother, Demeter, whose Roman counterpart is Ceres, the etymological namesake of our word *cereal*. The pinecone has been associated with Dionysus and his Roman counterpart Bacchus. The *Thyrsus*, which was a fennel staff woven with ivy and acanthus leaves and capped with a pinecone, was frequently depicted in Dionysian imagery. The pinecone atop the *Thrysus* was said to drip honey and was commonly used in Dionysian and Bacchic religious rites.

The Senior and Junior Deacon's rods are adorned with depictions of the Sun and Moon, respectively, within a square and compasses. This is mythologically significant in the case of the Senior Deacon who carries the Worshipful Masters' orders 'from East to West' – following, of course, the apparent path of the Sun from the perspective of the Earth. The Sun, which was universally anthropomorphized in ancient mythologies (as in the cases of Shamash, Ra, Horus, Helios, Phoebus-Apollo, Sol Invictus, et. al.), was made to occupy a solar barque or chariot during its diurnal circuit from East to West.[27]

By this analogy, it could easily be construed that the Junior Deacon's lunar symbolism is in relation to his position in the West of the Lodge – i.e. 'at the close of the day'. It is a common understanding, mythologically and otherwise, that the Sun is associated with the daytime and the Moon with the night – or, as it is stated in a certain Masonic lecture referencing the Three Lesser Lights of Freemasonry: "As the Sun rules the day and the Moon governs the night [...]".

Most mythological systems have some sort of lunar archetype – some with more developed narratives and attributes than others – to contrast and/or complement that of the solar. Some examples of these are Djehuti (Egyptian – an early, regional Thoth prototype whose attribution is lunar when depicted as an ibis or baboon with the Moon disc), Sin (Assyro-Babylonian), Cybele (Phrygian), the tripartite Hecate (Greek) and, of course, Luna (Roman).

---

27   Spence, *Ancient Egyptian Myths and Legends*, Barnes & Noble, 2005, pp. 105-106.

Hecate, the tripartite *Greek Goddess of the Crossroads*, Mallarmé, 1880

The crossed keys of the Treasurer's jewel are also a notable mythological motif, as they are also associated with the Anatolian, and later Greek, goddess Hecate[28], and also with the Leontocephaline, a lesser figure found in the iconography of Roman Mithraism.[29] Hecate, a lunar crone-goddess, was associated with crossroads, silver and currency – which is pertinent

28   Bulfinch, *Bulfinch's Mythology*, Barnes & Noble, 2006, pp. 130-131.
29   Cumont, *The Mysteries of Mithras*, Cosimo Classics, 2007, p. 105.

to the office of Treasurer. The Leontocephaline (who we will discuss in further detail in Section IV, which centers on Mithraism) is sometimes depicted with crossed keys held over the chest – in the manner of Osiris' ever-present crook and flail, which later morphed into general symbols of pharaonic authority – and a set of hammer and tongs, the working tools of Hephaestus, at his feet. This gains significance, Masonically, when we consider that Tubal-cain inhabits the same archetypal role in the Abrahamic canon (i.e. metallurgical artificer) as Hephaestus and Vulcan do in the Greek and Roman pantheons, respectively.[30] Notably, most depictions of the Leontocephaline also include the caduceus, or wand of Hermes. It is also suspected that this figure was a zoomorphic representation of the *Leo* Grade in the Mithraic initiatory cycle.[31]

The Leontocephaline

The Masonic Tyler's jewel, being a sword, is obviously a martial symbol. The Tyler's duties are, in part, "to keep off all cowans and eavesdroppers and see that none pass or repass [...]". In these regards, and considering the fact that the Tyler is sworn to guard and maintain the security of the Lodge, his office may be construed as the most aresian or martial. The jewel

30   Mackey, *The Symbolism of Freemasonry*, Forgotten Books, 2012, p. 361.
31   Cumont, *The Mysteries of Mithras*, Cosimo Classics, 2007, p. 105.

of the Lodge Historian – the quill and scrolled parchment – could easily be considered a modernized reworking of the ever-present stylus and papyrus of Thoth-Hermes, particularly in his chthonic role. As we have mentioned, Thoth was the designated scribe of the Egyptian *Ennead*. This also applies, albeit to a lesser extent, to the crossed quills of the Secretary's jewel.

The jewel of the Lodge Organist is the lyre and, therefore, has some of the most developed mythological significance. The lyre is most commonly associated with Orpheus, to whom it was given by Phoebus-Apollo (Apollo in his most solar aspect). Orpheus is said to have charmed man and beast with the instrument and to have used it to gain access to Hades in order to fetch Eurydice, his ill-fated bride. This he accomplished by enchanting both Charon, the Stygian boatman, and Cerberus, the three-headed dog, with his music.[32] The myth of his chthonic descent/ascent is said to have formed the basis of the Orphic Mysteries, which were an initiatory cycle in 6th Century Greece.[33] The influence of the Mystery Traditions, such as the Mithraic, Orphic and the Eleusinian, have been speculated to have survived in modern Freemasonry.[34] One may readily find depictions of the lyre in statuary and/or bas-relief adorning the many Orpheums and Lyric Halls across the Western World – these are, of course, in reference to Orpheus and his lyre, respectively.

THE MODES OF RECOGNITION

There is a body of signs, grips and words that form Freemasonry's Modes of Recognition. These are the signals by which Masons are differentiated from non-Masons. While it would, of course, be imprudent to explicitly reveal the words here, we may discuss their mythological import and those to whom the words have been given should be able to deduce the word in question.

There is a certain craftsmen archetype present in many mythological sets who is specifically associated with metallurgy. Hephaestus is perhaps the most well-known of this type. He was the only son produced by the union of Hera and Zeus and was the husband and half-brother of Aphrodite. His Roman counterpart was Vulcan. In the Abrahamic canon, this archetypal role was filled by the persona of Tubal-cain, who was referred to as "the forger of all instruments of bronze and iron"[35] and an "instructor of

32   Hamilton, *Mythology*, Grand Central, 2011, pp. 139-142.
33   Hutchens, *Pillars of Wisdom*, The Supreme Council A.A.S.R., 1995, pp. 128-131.
34   Vail, *The Ancient Mysteries and Modern Masonry*, Forgotten Books, 2012, p. 32.
35   Ibid.

every artificer in brass and iron."[36] Hephaestus, Vulcan and Tubal-cain were each associated with the making of weaponry and other martial attributes in scripture and epic poetry. The metallurgical arts practiced by these various mythological archetypes are a subset of the general body of alchemical arts, which figure prominently in the greater stream of Masonic tributaries.

Cybele, who was worshipped throughout the Roman empire as *Magna Mater* but was originally a Phrygian deity, was both a mother and a harvest goddess and the consort of Attis. Her name is similar, and may be etymologically related, to the Syrian word *sibola*, which means 'an ear of corn'.[37] This word, in turn, is reminiscent of the Ephraimitish pronunciation of the scriptural word *shibboleth*[38], which in modern times has come to mean: "a word or phrase frequently used, or a belief strongly held, by members of a group that is usually regarded by outsiders as meaningless, unimportant, or misguided."[39] The word *shibboleth* is associated with 'A sheaf of wheat (or, alternately, 'an ear of corn') hung by a water ford'. Cybele was not readily assimilated as a separate entity into the Hellenic pantheon due to her archetypal similarity to Demeter, the chief mother and harvest goddess, whose popular status was largely due to her exalted station in the Eleusinian Mysteries. Fittingly, the Eleusinian Mysteries were of the agricultural variety.

There is a tradition among Freemasons to identify themselves by the communication of a grip or token. This practice was carried over from the travelling operative stonemasons who utilized grips to signify their level of proficiency in the Craft, thereby entitling them to a certain wage or pay grade. Initiates into the Rites of Mithras were referred to as *syndexioi*, or 'fellows of the grip'[40], and admission into the fraternity was completed with a handshake with the *Pater* – a comparable office to the Worshipful Master of a Masonic Lodge. Mithras and the Sol Invictus were commonly represented performing this grip in bas-reliefs found in many *mithraeum* that have been discovered. This is, of course, Masonically significant particularly when we consider this grip vis-à-vis the Mithraic Grade of Leo, or Lion. The mythos and pantheon erected around the central figure of Mithras, himself a hermetic or mercurial archetype, included Sol Invictus (the 'Unconquerable Sun', an anthropomorphized solar deity), the Leontocephaline (the 'lion-headed', sphinxian personification of the Mithraic *Leo* grade), Cautes and Cautopates (the twin anthropomorphization of either

36   Ibid.
37   Brown, *Stellar Theology and Masonic Astronomy*, Merchant Books, 2008, pp. 73-74.
38   *The Holy Bible* KJV, Judges 12:6.
39   Encarta Dictionary, retrieved online.
40   Clauss, *The Roman Cult of Mithras*, Routledge, 2001, p. 42.

the equinoxes or the solstices, depending on the interpretation applied), and other lesser figures.

THE THREE LESSER LIGHTS

The Pythagorean Theorem, or the 47th Problem of Euclid, is also mentioned in a certain lecture in Masonic Ritual. There is some evidence to support the idea that the Three Lesser Lights should be situated around the alter in such a way as to form a 3:4:5, or Pythagorean Triangle; this depends, largely, on the dimensions of the Altar and the situation of the 'three burning tapers' that constitute the Three Lesser Lights. Generally, the altar is in the shape of an 'oblong square' (also called a 'double square', a quadrilateral equiangular rectangle with its broad sides being a 2:1 ratio to its narrow sides) and it is positioned in the center of the Lodge room with the broad sides facing East and West. In several states, the Three Lesser Lights are arranged in the Northwest, Southwest and Southeast around the altar. In this configuration, the Three Lesser Lights may be arranged to form a Pythagorean Triangle with the base *cathetus* facing West, the perpendicular *cathetus* facing South and the *hypotenuse* facing Northeast. The mythological attribution to this triangle is that the base represents Isis, the perpendicular Osiris, and the hypotenuse *Horus*.[41] The attribution of "the Sun, the Moon and the Master of the Lodge" to the three burning tapers surmounting the Lights at the angles of the triangle is addressed in Masonic ritual.

The Forty Seventh Problem – Higgins, *Hermetic Masonry*, Kessinger, 2012, p. 32

---

41   Clark, *The Royal Secret*, Kessinger, 2012, pp. 203-205.

THE BLAZING STAR

As mentioned in Section II of this volume, which dealt with the stellar relevance of Masonic symbolism, the Blazing Star has alternately been said to represent the Sun, Sirius (*A* and *B* combined, as seen by the naked eye) and Venus.[42] The Sun's significance as being the 'glory and beauty of the day', et cetera, is obvious and plainly stated in Masonic ritual but the theory of the Blazing Star as a representation of Sirius, or *Sothis*, as the star was known in Hellenistic Egypt, provides a much more interesting avenue of research, particularly when one considers the mythological significance of this star in world folklore.

Sirius, which is actually a binary system composed of the stars Sirius A and Sirius B, is the brightest star in the sky, apart from the Sun. This star resides in the constellation of *Canis Major*, hence the name 'the Dog Star' (a name from whence we get the phrase, 'the dog days of summer', or the Latin *dies caniculares*, denoting the heliacal rising and setting of Sirius during the summer months in that region). Interestingly, the canine associations are universally applied to Sirius in the stellar lore of the Northern Hemisphere. For instance, the Ancient Greeks called the star 'Orion's Dog'; in the mythology of the Pawnee tribe, and several other indigenous North American tribes, Sirius is referred to as the 'Wolf Star'; the Blackfoot referred to this star as 'Dog Face'; the Alaskan Inuits called it 'Moon Dog' and, in Chinese astronomy, Sirius is known as the 'Celestial Wolf'.

> *He was guided by one of the initiated, who wore a mask representing a dog's head in allusion to the bright star, Sothis, Sirius, or the dogstar, so called because the rising of that star each year above the horizon just before day gave warning of the approaching inundation of the Nile. The word Sothis means 'the barker' or 'monitor'.*[43]

Sirius, was especially significant to the agrarian cultures of the Nile River Valley due to the star's annual duty of heralding the coming inundation, which would eventually subside and leave the banks of the river fertile with silt. In light of the observational importance of this star, agriculturally, Sirius figured prominently in the symbolism and mythology of the region.[44]

---

42   Brown, *Stellar Theology and Masonic Astronomy*, Merchant Books, 2008, p. 59.
43   Clark, *The Royal Secret*, Kessinger, 2012, p. 7.
44   Hancock, *Fingerprints of the Gods*, Three Rivers, 1995, pp. 372-376.

Sirius was later personified as the Egyptian Iachen, the Minoan I Wa Ko and thereby the Greek Iakchos, or Iacchus, the torch-bearing son of Persephone.

CHTHONIC DESCENTS AND SOLAR ALLEGORIES

The descent into the Underworld is a culturally ubiquitous motif present in many world mythologies, occurring in the narratives of Ani/Osiris, Orpheus, Herakles, Aeneas, Persephone, and many others.[45] This may sometimes be interpreted as an allegorical representation of either night in the diurnal solar cycle, the winter solstice in the annual solar circuit, or representative of an agricultural cycle. Similarly, the ritual enactment of the Dying and Resurrecting God, as exemplified by the mortal initiate, is also a common feature in many initiatory systems.[46] The chthonic descent, or *katabasis*, as a liminal rite of initiation can be clearly discerned in the Egyptian *Book Of The Dead*, the Orphic Mysteries, the Eleusinian Mysteries, the Rites of Mithras and others. The hero descends into the Underworld to obtain a quest-object, where he may endure a type of judgement or ordeal, and typically ascends with a boon of some sort. The *katabasis* is a narrative device frequently employed in many Mystery systems and may be interpreted several ways; the most common of which are the solar, agricultural and psychological. Generally, there is also the presence of an eschatological theme such as metempsychosis or the immortality of the human soul.

The general narrative arc of the solar allegory, be it based upon the diurnal or the annual circuit, is a story to which we, as a people, have been exposed for millennia. Copious examples of the allegorically rendered solar circuit may also be discerned, in a myriad of variations within the body of world myth, fable, literature, and the arts in general.[47] This motif may be detected in such culturally and temporally diverse narratives as the Twelve Labors of Hercules, Samson and Delilah, the life and Ministry of Jesus Christ, the *Nibelungen* Cycle, *Cinderella*, the Samurai films of Akira Kurosawa, the 'Spaghetti Western' film genre, and even *Star Wars*, if one applies the appropriate interpretive keys. This narrative is ubiquitous for several reasons; two of the most common are its agricultural import, which is integral to civilization itself, and its psychological significance, which is embedded in mankind's collective unconscious.

---

45   Hamilton, *Mythology*, Grand Central, 2011, pp. 39-40.
46   Hall, *The Secret Teachings of All Ages*, Dover, 2010, pp. 195-197.
47   Hall, *The Secret Teachings of All Ages*, Dover, 2010, p. 186.

Herakles and the Cretan Bull, mosaic, may be interpreted as the
Sun in the House of Taurus

Herakles and the Nemean Lion, bas-relief, may be interpreted as the
Sun in the House of Leo

THE HIRAMIC LEGEND AS A MYTHOLOGICAL NARRATIVE

The second section of the Third Degree of Blue Lodge Freemasonry, or the Hiramic Legend, has been interpreted to be either an astrological or agricultural allegory, replete with a chthonic descent/ascent, along the lines of many similar initiatory structures in the Mystery Traditions of the Ancient Mediterranean and Near East.[48] These ritual dramas were universally based on regional variations on a common mythological narrative.

The Hiramic Legend follows the general narrative arc of a tragedy, as was common in the dramatic rituals of the Mysteries. We may consider the etymology of the word 'tragedy' in order to gain insight into these structures. The word τραγῳδία, or *tragōidia*, can be broken into its components which are *tragos*, meaning goat, and *ode*, or song. The literal interpretation of tragedy is 'goat song'.[49] Initially, the tragedies were relatively simple hymns to Pan, performed during the Dionysian or Bacchic Rites, but as these ritual dramatizations of folk mythological narratives developed in complexity of character, plot and performance, they gradually morphed into something recognizably closer to the modern conception of the theater. The Hiramic Legend certainly qualifies as a mythological narrative by this definition in that it is replete with its own archetypal characters and tragic plot-line that is highly allegorized and, thereby, subject to interpretation.

As an initiatory rite, the Hiramic Legend contains all of the necessary components to affect the transformation of the initiate central to such rites in all cultures. The persona of Hiram Abiff is first established as the vehicle for the consciousness of the initiate who portrays him in this cycle of transformation, as he is guided upon a 'perilous journey' by the Senior Deacon, who is here in his most hermetic, *psychopompic* role. This sequence is mirrored in many narratives in Classical Mythology, particularly those involving a quest or chthonic descent and a resultant boon that is retrieved from the Underworld. This sequence of Hiramic ritual-drama may be divided into the following acts:

---

48   Brown, *Stellar Theology and Masonic Astronomy*, Merchant Books, 2008, pp. 43-44.
49   Online Etymology Dictionary, *Tragedy*, etymonline.com, retrieved online.

1. The *Aphanism*. "In each of the initiations of the ancient Mysteries, there was a scenic representation of the death or disappearanceof some god or hero, whose adventures constituted the legend of the Mystery."[50] The death of and search for Hiram, in the Legend of the Third Degree.

2. The *Pastos*. "The coffin or grave which contained the body of the god or hero whose death was scenically represented in the ancient Mysteries."[51] This sequence corresponding to the *Katabasis*, or chthonic descent, as discussed earlier. Hiram is buried in the 'rubbish of the Temple' at 'Low Twelve'.

3. The *Euresis*. "That part of the initiation in the Ancient Mysteries which represented the finding of the body of the god or hero whose death and resurrection was the subject of the initiation."[52] This occurs when the Three Fellowcrafts discover the place of Hiram Abiff's interment, beneath the sprig of Acacia, which is itself a symbol of immortality.

4. The *Autopsy*. "The complete communication of the secrets in the ancient Mysteries, when the aspirant was admitted into the sacellum, or most sacred place, and was invested by the Hierophant with all the aporrheta, or sacred things, which constituted the perfect knowledge of the initiate."[53] This is represented by the *raising* of Hiram Abiff at 'High Twelve' and the investiture of the substitute Word, thereby officially appointing the initiate's newly elevated station.

> *The person thus slain was represented in the allegorical drama by the candidate. After the death followed the disappearance of the body, called by the Greeks the aphanism, and the consequent search for it. This search for the body, in which all the initiates joined, constituted what Faber calls "the doleful part," and was succeeded by its discovery, which was known as the heuresis. This was accompanied by the greatest demonstrations of joy. The candidate was afterward instructed in the*

---

50   Mackey, *The Symbolism of Freemasonry*, Forgotten Books, 2012, p. 317.
51   ibid. p. 352.
52   Ibid. p. 334.
53   Ibid. p. 322.

apporheta, or secret dogmas of the Mysteries. In all of the Pa-
gan Mysteries this dramatic form of an allegory was preserved,
and we may readily see in the groans and lamentations on the
death of the god or hero and the disappearance of the body a
symbol of the death of man, and in the subsequent rejoicings at
his discovery and restoration, a symbol of the restoration of the
spirit to eternal life.[54]

In anthropological terms, these events correspond to those in liminal (from the Latin *limen*, or threshold) rites of passage. Patterns of initiations such as the rite of separation (pre-liminal), the rite of transition (liminal), and the rite of reincorporation (post-liminal)[55] are all integral to Masonic initiatory rituals. The candidate is sequestered and subjected to a species of deprivation; he is then guided through a transformational ordeal resulting in the 'death' of his former self; and he is finally reintegrated with his peers, having effectively arrived at his new station in life.

In terms of comparative mythology, the initiatory pattern of the Hiramic Legend may also be examined vis-à-vis Joseph Campbell's hero's journey, which is a segment of his greater monomyth. The hero – in this sense, the narrative's protagonist – is compelled on a journey, quest or adventure whereupon he encounters a crisis or ordeal. He eventually overcomes the obstacle and returns home transformed. Campbell, who was influenced by Jung's interpretations of myth, posited that this cycle was a common template found in a wide array of world mythology and folklore and that, further, this transformational cycle has its origin in the primordial psyche of mankind.

THE WEEPING VIRGIN OF THE THIRD DEGREE

The Weeping Virgin of the Third Degree is a statue made reference to in the Master Mason Lecture in Blue Lodge Freemasonry. The work consists of the figure of a virgin, her hands folded as in prayer, leaning over a broken column as an old man, holding a scythe, undoes the braids in her hair. There are several mythological allusions in this arrangement that readily present themselves to the mind. The old, male figure bears a likeness to Cronus (Saturn), the Titanic father of Zeus (Jupiter), pres-

---

54 Mackey, *The History of Freemasonry*, Grammercy, 1996, p. 185.
55 See: van Gennep's *Rites of Passage*, 1906, and Turner's *The Forest of Symbols*, 1967.

ent here in his popular personification as Father Time. The weeping virgin, in this context, could be construed as a representation of Persephone (Proserpina), the *kore*.

In this interpretation, we are reminded of an incident in Greek Mythology known as the *Rape of Persephone*. There are both astrological and agricultural keys to the allegory of this event and these, when used in conjunction, provide us with an interesting narrative. If we consider the figure of Father Time as representing Saturn then, through common and established astrological correspondences, we arrive at the winter solstice via the zodiacal house of Capricornus, which is ruled by Saturn. In the myth, Persephone was abducted by Hades while she was collecting wild flowers – an obvious sign of spring or the vernal equinox. He then carried her to his kingdom in the Underworld, which is also symbolic of the winter solstice – a place almost universally regarded as the abode of death. The whole scene can easily be read as a depiction of certain known aspects of the Eleusinian Mysteries[56], which were both agricultural (and thereby, solar) and, perhaps, entheogenic [Before breaking their fast and proceeding into the Greater Mysteries of Eleusis, initiates were asked, "Have you drank the Kykeon?" The *Kykeon* is conjectured to have been a barley-based, entheogenic brew, wherein the barley had been allowed to be parasitized by ergot, the psycho-active properties of fungus. This would have prepared the initiates for the concluding revelations of these Mysteries. Though little is definitively known of these Mysteries, due to strict vows of secrecy, it has been said that initiates were shown "an ear of corn, in silence reaped." The significance of this passage should not be lost on those who have been passed to the degree of Fellowcraft.].

---

56   Graves, *The White Goddess*, FSG Classics, 2013, pp. 152-154.

The Beautiful Virgin of the Third Degree – Brown, *Stellar Theology and Masonic Astronomy,*
Merchant, 2008, p. 69

CONCLUSION OF SECTION III

The mythologies and folk narratives of the world continue to inspire us and to provide subtextual buoyancy to our experiences today, aesthetic and otherwise. In terms of Jungian psychology, myth and folklore may unite us with latent and vestigial aspects of ourselves. We encounter archetypal characters such as the *Anima/Animus*, the *Wise Old Man* or the *Shadow Self*, for example, and we are thereby given the opportunity to integrate these elements into a coherent whole – the *Individuated Self*. Anthropologically, world mythologies remain a cultural touchstone, inextricably linking us with the minds and imaginations of our ancient forebears from the dawn of human civilization – nay, the dawn of the human psyche itself.

The fact that these ancient personas and narratives are still charged with meaning, and that they continue to develop in proportion to our understanding of our collective experience of the world, surely places mythology as a living tradition, capable of providing us with valuable insights. When we consider these factors in the context of Freemasonry, we come to understand another facet of our eminent fraternity. Albert Pike, in reference to this priceless heritage inherited by Freemasonry wrote, "And so I came at last to see that the true greatness and majesty of Freemasonry consist in its proprietorship of these and its other symbols; and that its symbolism is its soul."[57] Similarly, Manly P. Hall, in his 1928 work *The Secret Teachings of All Ages*, wrote, "A hundred religions have brought their gifts of wisdom to [Freemasonry's] altar; arts and sciences unnumbered have contributed to its symbolism."

So, at last, in Classical Mythology, we find yet another lens through which to view and interpret the symbolism of Freemasonry. It seems that no matter which lens we apply – the philosophical, the mathematical, the astrological and, presently, the mythological – Freemasonry stands up to the most intense scrutiny as being more than just, "a peculiar system of morality, veiled in allegory and illustrated by symbols."

---

57   Pike, excerpt from *Letter to Gould*, via sacred-texts.com, retrieved online.

Greek theater mask, *Prosopon* in Greek - *Persona* in Latin, from whence we get
the term for the outward aspects of our character

SECTION IV:

FREEMASONRY AND
THE RITES OF MITHRAS

FREEMASONRY AND THE RITES OF MITHRAS

"Some claim that various traditions of Scottish Freemasonry can even be traced back to Mithraism. The 'painted' tribesman or Picti of Scotland would have encountered Mithraea of the Roman soldiers along Hadrian's Wall. Since they remained outside the Empire, the Christian conversion would have left them unchanged."[1]

It has been regularly posited throughout the history of Masonic scholarship that some of the customs, ritualism and initiatic content present in modern Freemasonry has its origins in remote antiquity, as certain aspects of these rituals find an antecedent in several ancient Mystery Religions.[2][3][4] Chief among these prospective contributors is Mithraism – specifically, the initiatory rites and associated customs practiced by the Roman Legionaries in the first few centuries of the 1st Millennium CE.

It is the primary purpose of this Section of the present work to illuminate and examine a selection of the more significant examples of the many correspondences that exist between Freemasonry and the Rites of Mithras.

As before, and in order to formulate a coherent contextual basis, a brief exposition of both Freemasonry and Mithraism will first be necessary before we can begin to effectively collate these correspondences. This will serve simultaneously as a definition of our terms and as an orientation to the further comparison and juxtaposition of our subjects.

---

1   Ruck, Hoffman and Celdran, *Mushrooms, Myths and Mithras*, City Lights, 2011.
2   Vail, *The Ancient Mysteries and Modern Masonry*, Forgotten Books, 2012, p. 9.
3   Hall, *The Secret Teachings of All Ages*, Dover, 2010, p. 516.
4   Mackey, *The Symbolism of Freemasonry*, Forgotten Books, 2012, p. 39.

OPERATIVE AND SPECULATIVE FREEMASONRY

As we have outlined in Section I, Freemasonry is generally considered to consist of two subsets – the operative and the speculative Craft. At one time, these were one and the same. However, the differentiation of these aspects of the Craft is relatively complete, having been underway for at least three centuries with the gradual admission of speculative Masons, alternately known as Accepted Masons, into the guilds of the operative Craft.[5]

Operative Freemasonry refers to the actual trade practices of stone-masonry such as quarrying, preparing, setting and finishing free stone in accordance with an architectural design. This practice is of extreme antiquity, as there are many examples of edifices across the globe that are estimated to have been constructed at the dawn of the Neolithic Era (commencing around 10,500 BCE), not long after the last glacial thaw, occurring at the close of the Epipaleolithic Period.[6] Many of these megalithic structures were conceived, designed and erected with a level of proficiency that, in many cases, has never been surpassed. Often, a very developed conception of proportion, geometry and astronomy are discerned in these ancient edifices – sometimes causing us to revise some of our most fundamental anthropological ideas, as was the case concerning the relatively recent discovery of the temple complex at Göbekli Tepe.[7]

Some of the very early guilds of stonemasons, such as the Dionysian Artificers and the Roman *Collegia*, were believed to have perpetuated not only the trade secrets of the operative Craft, but also those secrets which are suspected to have been inculcated in several of the Ancient Mystery Traditions; conspicuously.[8] Specifically, this would account for the undiluted and undiffused transmission of the requisite practical and theoretical knowledge of geometry and astronomy necessary for the construction of the sort of astrologically-aligned structures we find. Later, the Lombard stonemasons of the Middle Ages, such as the *Magistri Comacini* and the *Maestri Campionesi*, represented a continuation of these concerns in the operative Craft.[9]

The fact that the Masons who populated the aforementioned guilds

---

5   Ibid. p. 63.
6   Scham, *The World's First Temple*, Archaeology Magazine, Dec. 2008, p. 23.
7   Ibid. p. 23.
8   Mackey, *The History of Freemasonry*, Kessinger, 2012, p. 485.
9   Haywood, *The Builder* Magazine, Volume IX - Number 10, *Part VI. Freemasonry and the Comacine Masters*, retrieved online.

were free to travel and had also been invested with a body of information which constituted the operative trade secrets of the time – in addition to those skills associated with the Boethius' *Quadrivium* – proved to be attractive to the intellectuals, alchemists, would-be Rosicrucians and miscellaneous freethinkers of the Enlightenment Era who composed the initial swell of Accepted initiates.[10] That these Mysteries were kept inviolate, and that men were allowed to learn and utilize them at all, was very significant considering the establishment of the Inquisitorial Courts, whose purpose it was to combat heresy. While the rampant and unchecked oppression of the Inquisitions has not shone kindly in the historical view of the Roman Catholic Church, it should be noted that this period provided fertile ground for the mercurial rise experienced in the Western World, heralded by the Enlightenment.[11]

Speculative Masonry utilizes the hierarchical structure, working tools and vernacular of operative stonemason's guilds, in addition to various aspects of the Old Testament narrative of the building of King Solomon's Temple, in a fraternal order whose principal tenets are *brotherly love*, *relief* and *truth*. Masons are *made* via the employment of initiatory rites which are designed to inculcate moral and ethical lessons in the mind of the initiate. These allegorical rites of initiation, or Degrees, constitute the Fraternity's primary method of instruction.

MITHRAISM

Mithraism was a Mystery religion influenced by 6th century BCE Persian Zoroastrianism, the astrolatric tradition of the Chaldean astronomers and the Persian *magi*, as discussed in Section I. It had a fraternal, initiatory Grade system and was the preferred cult of the Roman Legionaries.[12] Most of what we have come to know of this initiatory tradition comes from the study of extant bas-relief, statuary, fragments and graffiti found on the walls of the cult's grotto temples, known as *mithraea*. Beyond these scraps of data, little is known of this once very powerful and influential fraternal order that was believed to be early Christianity's biggest rival for the collective soul of the Roman Empire.

---

10   Mackey, *The Symbolism of Freemasonry*, Forgotten Books, 2012, p. 63.

11   Encyclopedia Britannica Inc., *Enlightenment*, britannica.com, 2016, retrieved online.

12   Graves, *The White Goddess*, FSG Classics, 2013, p. 204.

Mithraeum, Basilica Saint Clement, Rome

THE CORRESPONDENCES BETWEEN
FREEMASONRY AND THE RITES OF MITHRAS

As we examine the body of correspondences existing between Free-masonry and Mithraism, it is important to bear in mind that it is not the purpose of this work to endeavor to establish an uninterrupted lineage, nor to imply any kind of direct cultural inheritance – an argument of this sort would, of course, require a detailed anthropological study beyond the scope of the present work – we are merely highlighting a set of commonalities which, it is hoped, will serve to provide substance for further contemplation. That being said, notable Masonic scholars such as Mackey, Pike, Oliver and Vail have examined and subsequently done much to buttress such an idea.

> *The Rev. Mr. King, the author of a very interesting treatise on the Gnostics, has advanced a theory much more plausible than either of those to which I have adverted. He maintains that some of the Pagan Mysteries, especially those of Mithras, which had been instituted in Persia, extended beyond the period of the advent of Christianity, and that their doctrines*

and usages were adopted by the secret societies which existed at an early period in Europe and which finally assumed the form of Freemasonry. I have said that this theory is a plausible one. It is so because its salient points are sustained by historical evidence.[13]

Like the Masonic Lodge, the Mithraic grotto, or *mithraeum*, was known to be a microcosmic representation of the universe[14] and, similarly, there are many signs and symbols of a generally astrological character. "The ceiling of the *Caesarea Maritima Mithraeum* retains traces of blue paint, which may mean the ceiling was painted to depict the sky and the stars."[15] *Mithraea* were also windowless, as are most Masonic Lodge rooms.

The Mithraic Grade structure was often represented by a seven-runged ladder which also corresponded to the seven classical planets (those visible to the ancients in the absence of telescopic aid – the Sun, the Moon, Mars, Mercury, Jupiter, Venus and Saturn).[16] This finds a parallel in the Masonic Lodge with the representation of Jacob's Ladder and, to a lesser extent, the third flight of stairs in a certain 'Winding Staircase' leading to the M.C. of K.S.T., which is mentioned in a lecture pertaining to the Degree of Fellowcraft. This flight of stairs consists of seven steps which directly correspond to the seven liberal arts and sciences, or the *Trivium* (grammar, rhetoric and logic) and *Quadrivium* (arithmetic, geometry, music and astronomy).

Each Mithraic Grade also had a set of symbolic implements that functioned as mnemonic cues to the teachings and basic tenets associated with the corresponding Grade. This practice also finds a correlation in the speculative application of the Working Tools associated with each Masonic Degree. For instance, the beaker and *caduceus* were attributed to the Grade of *Corax*, the first Mithraic Grade[17]; while, in Freemasonry, the Twenty-four Inch Gauge and the Common Gavel are assigned to the Entered Apprentice, or First Degree. The Grades of Mithraism are believed to have been as follows (listed here, in ascending order, with their translations and symbolic implements):

13   Mackey, *The History of Freemasonry*, Grammercy, 1996, pp. 190-191.

14   Pike, *Morals and Dogma*, L. H. Jenkins Inc., 1947, p. 413.

15   Hopfe, *Archaeological indications on the origins of Roman Mithraism*, Rosicrucian Digest No. 2, AMORC, 2008, p. 21.

16   Pike, *Morals and Dogma*, L. H. Jenkins Inc., 1947, p. 11.

17   Chalupa, *Seven Mithraic Grades: An Initiatory or Priestly Hierarchy?*, academia.edu, 2008, retrieved online.

Corax (crow - beaker and *caduceus*)
Nymphus (bridegroom - lamp, bell and veil)
Miles (soldier - helmet, lance and drum)
Leo (lion - *sistrum*, laurel wreath and thunderbolts)
Perses (Persian - Phrygian cap and sickle)
Heliodromus (sun-runner - torch, Helios' whip and robes)
Pater (father - mitre, shepherd's staff and garnet ring)

There was also an oath, or obligation, associated with each of the seven Grade conferrals. "Mithraic initiates were required to swear an oath of secrecy and dedication, and some Grade rituals involved the recital of a catechism, wherein the initiate was asked a series of questions pertaining to the initiation symbolism and had to reply with specific answers."[18] Fragments of an obligation and catechism, presumably from the Mithraic Grade of Leo have been discovered. The catechism is similar in form to those found in Masonic degrees, replete with instructional precepts and recapitulations of the events in the ritual to which it pertains. Like a Masonic catechism, it is composed in fixed question-and-answer form. In one portion of the fragment, the initiator (probably, the *Heliodromus*) asks, "How did you become a *Leo*?" to which the initiate replies, "By the [order] of the *Pater*."[19]

> He will say: 'Where [...]?' Say: 'Night'.
> (He will say): '... you are called ...?' Say: 'Because of the summery [...]'
> [...] having become [...] he/it has the fiery [...]
> (He will say): '[...] did you receive/inherit?' Say: 'In a pit'.
> He will say: 'Where is your [...]? (Say): '[...] (in the) Leonteion'.
> He will say: 'Will you gird?' The (heavenly?) (Say): '[...] death'.
> He will say: 'Why, having girded yourself, [...]?'
> He will say: 'Who is the father?' Say: 'The one who (begets?) everything'
> He will say: '('How?') did you become a Leo?' Say: 'By the [...] of the father'.[20]

---

18   Geden, *Select Passages Illustrating Mithraism,* Kessinger, 1925, p. 51.
19   See: third century *Oxyrhynchus* papyrus which was published by Bartoletti as n. 1162 in *Papiri, Greci e Latini.*
20   Brashear, *A Mithraic Catechism from Egypt,* Vienna: Holzhausen, 1992 – 18.5.

Mithraic initiates were permitted to travel to, and affiliate with, *mithraea* other than that in which they were initiated – much like the privileges modern Masons, who are sometimes referred to as 'Travelling Men', enjoy. Similar to the self-governing modern Masonic Lodges, each *mithraea* functioned autonomously. "Each *Mithraeum* had its own officers and functionaries [and] there was no central supervisory authority [...] It is known that initiates could transfer with their Grades from one *Mithraeum* to another."[21] The establishment of a new *mithraea* was often precipitated by the overflow of membership from those nearby that had become filled to capacity; this is known to have occurred in Freemasonry at the height of the Age of Fraternalism, when the Craft's popularity was at its peak. It also appears that, though the presence of iconography such as the *Tauroctony* and the Leontocephaline was exceedingly common from *mithraea* to *mithraea*, each individual *mithraeum* had no organized and dogmatic central teaching, *per se*, other than that which was inculcated in their rituals.[22]

As we have mentioned in the foregoing, Mithraic initiates were sometimes referred to as *syndexioi*, or 'fellows of the grip'[23] and it is noted that admission into the community was completed with a handshake with the *Pater* (comparable to the Worshipful Master of the Masonic Lodge), just as Mithras and the Sol Invictus were represented as doing in a common motif found in many of the extant Mithraic bas-reliefs. This is, of course, Masonically significant particularly when we consider the significance of this grip in the context of the Mithraic Grade of Leo, or Lion, for reasons any Master Mason can readily deduce, though we cannot be sure that there were specific grips corresponding to each grade, as in Blue Lodge Freemasonry.

Adherents to the earlier forms of Persian mysticism (commonly collected under the general banner of Magianism) that birthed the theological, philosophical and astrological systems that would become Zoroastrianism and, eventually, Mithraism were called *magi*. This word is an etymological tributary to the word Magic.[24] The Latin singular form for *magi* is *magus* – an appellation which has made several appearances in the Grade hierarchies of various Rosicrucian and hermetic orders – firstly, and most notably, in the Masonic invitational order, *Societas Rosicruciana* (known in the United States as the SRICF, or *Societas Rosicruciana in Civitatibus Foederatis*), founded in the mid-19th Century.

21   Clauss, *The Roman cult of Mithras*, Routledge, 2001, p. 139.
22   Beck, *The Religion of the Mithras Cult in the Roman Empire*, Oxford University Press, 2007, p. 87.
23   Clauss, *The Roman Cult of Mithras*, Routledge, 2001, p. 42.
24   Online Etymology Dictionary, *Magic*, etymonline.com, retrieved online.

THE ANNO LUCIS AND THE TAUROCTONY

As we have discussed, the first *Anno Lucis* of Freemasonry, considered in regard to axial precession, would have occurred in proximity to the dawn of the Taurian Age, which spanned from approximately 4000 to 2000 BCE. Mithraism is laden with Taurian imagery, as evidenced in nearly every extant grotto, and it is suggested that the *Tauroctony* – a depiction of *Mithras*, rendered here as a solar anthropomorphism, surmounting and slaying a bull – is often interpreted to be a symbolic representation of the vernal equinox occurring in the zodiacal house of Taurus[25], thus harkening back to the very same period as that of the Masonic *Anno Lucis*.

In the *Tauroctony*, embordering the central equinoctial figuration of Mithras and the Taurian Bull, there are depictions of the torchbearers Cautes and Cautopates. These characters, cross-legged and dressed in distinctly Anatolian garb, have been interpreted as solstitial representations[26], as have the Saints John via the two parallel, perpendicular lines – one ascribed with a letter *B* for John the Baptist and the other with a letter *E* for John the Evangelist – in the Masonic Point Within A Circle diagram.[27]

Tauroctony, Mithraeum at Circus Maximus, underground Mithraic temple, Rome

The Leontocephaline, a lion-headed figure commonly represented in Mithraic bas-relief and statuary, is often depicted as being spirally entwined

25   Pike, *Morals and Dogma*, L. H. Jenkins Inc., 1947, p. 413.
26   Ruck, Hoffman and Celdran, *Mushrooms, Myths and Mithras*, City Lights, 2011, p. 60.
27   Mackey, *The Symbolism of Freemasonry*, Forgotten Books, 2012, p. 115.

by one, and sometimes two serpents. The figure is also frequently represented as holding two crossed keys, similar to the Jewel of the Treasurer of the
Masonic Lodge. Notably, this zoomorphic representation of the *Leo* Grade
often included a hammer and tongs at his feet.[28] These metallurgical instruments, particularly in the Roman Empire, were commonly associated with
Vulcan who, through syncretization, was also associated with Hephaestus in the Hellenic pantheon and Tubal-cain in the Abrahamic canon.[29]

Oftentimes, the cock and the *caduceus*, both associated with Mercury,
are also found at the base of the statue. Interestingly, both of these symbols are sometimes found in the Masonic Chamber of Reflection (a space
utilized for the *rite of separation* in the liminal model of initiation, found in
some Masonic Lodges, intended to provide an environment conducive to
the generation of a contemplative or receptive consciousness in the candidate for initiation[30], where they are often explained vis-à-vis their alchemical import. The cock, when taken in the context present in this total body of
symbols, is reminiscent of the sphinxian, or polymorphic figure of Abrasax,
the primary deific image in the 2nd century CE Basilidian Gnostic sect.
Abrasax (also Abraxas) is usually depicted as having the head of a cock,
two serpents for legs and human arms usually holding a flail and the reins
of a chariot. Strengthening the Gnostic hypothesis, somewhat, is the theory that the Leontocephaline is the demiurge, Ialdabaoth[31]; a lion-headed figure, generally depicted with solar corona and the body of a serpent.

Abrasax, or Abraxas, depicted
on a Gnostic talisman

Ialdabaoth depicted
on a Gnostic talisman

28   Cumont, *The Mysteries of Mithras*, Cosimo Classics, 2007, p. 105.
29   Mackey, *The Symbolism of Freemasonry*, Forgotten Books, 2012, p. 361.
30   Martinez, *The Anteroom or Chamber of Reflection*, freemasoninformation.com, 2009,
retrieved online.
31   Gwynn, *Religious diversity in late antiquity*, Brill, 2010, p. 448.

There is evidence that many Mithraic rituals and ceremonies were accompanied by, or culminated in a ritual feast.[32] High concentrations of cherry stones have been observed at various *mithraea*, pointing to a feasting period of late June through early July – this period, of course, contains the summer solstice. This projected seasonal time frame has been corroborated by the *Virunum* album which records a Mithraic feast as having occurred on June 26th, 184 CE; comfortably within the period of the summer solstice.[33] Solstitial feasts of this kind were and are relatively common in pagandom. The feasts of both Saint John the Baptist and Saint John the Evangelist, respectively corresponding to the summer and winter solstices, are still a relatively common practice, particularly among Masons.

SOLAR ALLEGORY AND RITUAL DRAMA

The Mithraic Grade of *Miles* is said to have consisted of the performance of a solar allegory represented in a ritual drama, wherein the initiate was said to descend into the grotto via the gate of Cancer (representing the summer solstice – and, thereby, also notable as a possible annual counterpart to the diurnal 'High Twelve' in the Hiramic Legend of Freemasonry), where he passed through the spheres of the Seven Classical Planets. While in this chthonic realm, the *Miles*, after having adopted a quality of each planetary sphere through which he had passed, was subjected to the judgement of *Mithras*. He was then purged of the qualities he had collected during his descent by the performance of Seven Sacraments and made his exit via the gate of Capricorn (the winter solstice, or 'Low Twelve' in the analogous Masonic allegory). "[The] Procession of the Sun-Runner [initiatory ritual] features the *Heliodromus*, escorted by two figures representing Cautes and Cautopates and preceded by an initiate of the Grade *Miles* leading a ritual enactment of the solar journey around the *Mithraeum*, which was intended to represent the cosmos."[34] A similarly allegorical solar interpretation has also been applied, very compellingly, to the Hiramic Legend in Masonic Ritual.[35]

---

32   Clauss, *The Roman Cult of Mithras*, Routledge, 2001, p. 115.
33   Beck, Beck on Mithraism, Ashgate Publishing, 2004, p. 335.
34   Martin, *Ritual Competence and Mithraic Ritual*, 2004, p. 257.
35   Brown, Stellar Theology and Masonic Astronomy, Merchant Books, 2008, pp. 43–44.

CONCLUSION OF SECTION IV

While it may be impossible to trace anything like a direct and un-broken lineage spanning from Mithraism to Freemasonry, the former, as it was found in the first few centuries of the first millennium CE, contained many customs, protocols and practices that bring to mind those observed in the constitution, landmarks and ritualism of the latter. It is hoped that the information presented in the foregoing will provide ample substance for contemplation and the impetus for further independent research into the Rites of Mithras and other possible tributaries to the Mysteries of Freemasonry.

BIBLIOGRAPHY

Aveni, *In Search of Ancient Astronomies*, Doubleday, 1978

Barnstone and Meyer (editors), *The Gnostic Bible*, Shambhala, 2009

Beck, *Beck on Mithraism,* Ashgate Publishing, 2004

Beck, *The Religion of the Mithras Cult in the Roman Empire,* Oxford University Press, 2007

Brown, *Stellar Theology and Masonic Astronomy*, Merchant Books, 2008

Budge, *The Gods of the Egyptians,* vol. 1, Dover, 2013

Budge, *The Gods of the Egyptians*, vol. 2, Dover, 2013

Bulfinch, *Bulfinch's Mythology*, Barnes & Noble, 2006

Campbell, *The Hero with a Thousand Faces*, Bollingen, 1973

Carter, *An Introduction to Political Astrology (Mundane Astrology)*, Camelot Press, 1973

Case, *Occult Fundamentals and Spiritual Unfoldment: Early Writings Vol. 1*, Fraternity of the Hidden Light, 2008

Chevalier, et. al., *Penguin Dictionary of Symbols*, Penguin, 1997

Clark, *The Royal Secret*, Kessinger, 2012

Clauss, *The Roman Cult of Mithras*, Routledge, 2001

Crowley, *Liber ABA: Book 4*, Weiser, 2008

Crowley, *Gems from the Equinox*, Weiser, 2007

Cumont, *The Mysteries of Mithras*, Cosimo Classics, 2007

DuQuette, *The Chicken Qabalah*, Weiser, 2001

DuQuette, *The Key to Solomon's Key*, CCC Publishing, 2010

Fortune, *The Mystical Qabalah*, Weiser, 1998

Frazer, *The Golden Bough*, Oxford, 2009

Geden, *Select Passages Illustrating Mithraism,* Kessinger, 1925

Gilles, *The Way of Hermes: New Translations of The Corpus Hermeticum,* Inner Traditions, 2004

Graves, *The White Goddess*, FSG Classics, 2013

Gwynn, *Religious diversity in late antiquity,* Brill, 2010

Hall, *The Secret Teachings of All Ages*, Dover, 2010

Hamilton, *Mythology*, Grand Central, 2011

Hancock, *Fingerprints of the Gods*, Three Rivers, 1995

Higgins, *AUM: The Lost Word,* Kessinger, 2012

Higgins, *Hermetic Masonry*, Kessinger, 2012

Hutchens, *Pillars of Wisdom,* The Supreme Council A.A.S.R., 1995

Jung, *Collected Works*, Bollingen, 1968

Jung, *Man and His Symbols*, Doubleday, 1964

Jung, *Psychology and Alchemy*, Routledge and Kegan Paul, 1953

Kaczynski, *Perdurabo: The Life of Aleister Crowley,* North Atlantic, 2010

Kaczynski, *Forgotten Templars: The Untold Origins of Ordo Templi Orientis,* Kaczynski, 2012

Kraig, *Modern Magick*, Llewellyn, 1994

Levi, *Transcendental Magic: Its Doctrine and Ritual*, Martino Publishing, 2011

Mackey, *The History of Freemasonry,* Grammercy, 1996

Mackey, *The Symbolism of Freemasonry*, Forgotten Books, 2012

Mathers, *The Key of Solomon the King*, Weiser, 2006

Mathers/Crowley, *The Goetia*, Weiser, 1997

McCluskey, *Time and Astronomy in Past Cultures*, Gorgias Press, 2006

Newman, *Alchemically Stoned,* The Laudable Pursuit, 2017

Nichols, *Jung and Tarot*, Weiser, 1984

Nilsson, *Greek Popular Religion*, Bibliolife, 2009

Pike, *Morals and Dogma*, L. H. Jenkins Inc., 1947

Regardie, *The Golden Dawn*, Llewellyn, 2014

Ruck, Hoffman and Celdran, *Mushrooms, Myths and Mithras*, City Lights, 2011

Spence, *Ancient Egyptian Myths and Legends*, Barnes & Noble, 2005

Three Initiates, *The Kybalion*, Yogi Publication Society Masonic Temple, 1912

Vail, *The Ancient Mysteries and Modern Masonry*, Forgotten Books, 2012

Vitruvius, *De Architectura*, Penguin, 2009

The Holy Bible KJV

Official Masonic Ritual, Grand Lodge of Connecticut, 2010

New Larousse *Encyclopedia of Mythology*, Hamlyn Publishing Group, 1972

INDEX

Symbols

47th Proposition of Euclid 11

A

A∴A∴ 21
Abiff, Hiram 6, 33, 66, 67, 69, 70, 82, 83, 84, 97, 98
Abracadabra 17
Abramelin, Book of 16, 17
Abramelin, Oil of 16, 17
Abraxas 117
Acacia 66, 67, 70, 71, 72, 83, 84, 98
Aeneas 95
Alchemy 8, 11, 15, 23, 42, 62
Alpha et Omega 23
Amalthea 88
Androsphinxes 31, 46, 56
Angels 8
Anno Lucis 45, 46, 53, 58, 69, 72, 84, 116
Aphrodite 82, 91
Apollo 88, 91
Archetypes 78, 85, 92
Astrology 8, 11, 23, 42, 56
Astronomy 8, 11, 19, 42, 50, 51, 52, 65, 94, 110, 113
Athena 77, 82
AUM 71
Axial Precession 45, 47, 49, 53, 116

B

Blazing Star 57, 61, 62, 94
Brazen Pillars 11, 13, 59, 72, 83, 84
Builders of the Adytum 23

C

Campbell, Joseph 80, 81, 85, 99
Caput Mortuum 15
Case, Paul Foster 23, 56, 72
Cautes and Cautopates 46, 47, 92, 116, 118
Cerberus 91
Ceremonial Magick 3, 4, 7, 8, 9, 11, 13, 14, 16, 20, 21, 23, 25, 27, 29, 31, 34, 36, 37
Chamber of Reflection 15, 28, 117
Charon 91

Checkered Pavement 61
Christianity 111, 112
Circumambulation 29, 47, 48, 59, 86
Clement of Alexandria 87
Collegia 50, 110
Cronus 99
Crowley, Aleister 7, 13, 16, 17, 21, 27, 29
Cybele 88, 92

D

Daedalus 84
Daemons 8, 27
Degrees 5, 20, 22, 43, 45, 49, 54, 62, 114
Demeter 85, 88, 92
Dionysus 88
Djinn 8

E

Ecclesia Gnostica Catholica 17
Egregore 15, 17, 28
Elements, Four Classical 30
Eleusinian Mysteries 28, 69, 92, 95, 100
Emerald Tablet 10, 47, 48
Entered Apprentice 5, 72, 113
Entheogens 44
Equinoxes 30, 46, 47, 49, 50, 56, 58, 61, 69, 93
Evocation 15, 27, 31
Ezekiel's Vision 30, 56

F

Fellowcraft 5, 11, 14, 50, 66, 69, 72, 82, 83, 86, 100, 113
Fichtuld, Hermann 24
Frazer, J. G. 79, 81
Freemasonry 41, 42, 45, 46, 48, 49, 50, 53, 54, 58, 60, 63, 64, 65, 68, 73, 78, 81,
    82, 84, 85, 87, 88, 90, 91, 97, 98, 99, 103, 109, 110, 111, 112, 113, 115,
    116, 117, 118, 119

G

Geometry 4, 11, 19, 42, 44, 49, 50, 51, 52, 65, 110, 113
Gnosis 34
Gnostic 47, 117
God Forms 21

Goetia 27
Golden Age of Fraternalism 8
Grades 24, 25, 43, 45, 113, 115
Grand Architect of the Universe 15
Grimoire 16, 27

H

Hades 29, 79, 83, 85, 86, 91, 100
Hall, Manly P. 14, 16, 23, 29, 30, 47, 59, 60, 69, 87, 95, 103, 109
Hecate 88, 89
Helios 88, 114
Hephaestus 90, 91, 92, 117
Hera 83, 91
Herakles 83, 84, 85, 95, 96
Hermes 4, 10, 12, 47, 85, 86, 87, 90, 91
Hermes Trismegistus 4, 10, 47, 87
Hermeticism 3, 10, 23, 34
Hermetic Order of the Golden Dawn 3, 9, 23, 24, 25, 31
Hiramic Legend 29, 33, 47, 65, 67, 69, 86, 97, 99, 118
Holy Bible 11, 16, 30, 56, 59, 70, 83, 92
Holy Guardian Angel 18, 21, 34
Hoodwink 28
Horus 69, 88, 93
Hypnosis 18

I

Ialdabaoth 117
Iliad 87
Individuation 21, 34
Initiation 3, 15, 20, 28, 33, 43, 45, 59, 78, 84, 95, 98, 111, 114, 117
Invocation 28
Isis 12, 69, 70, 71, 93

J

Jacob's Ladder 36, 45, 113
Jason 84
Jesus 18, 62, 72, 95
Jung, Carl Gustav 16, 18, 19, 20, 21, 79, 81, 87, 99

K

Kabbalah 22, 23
King Hiram of Tyre 6, 67

Kybalion 4, 12, 47

L

Leontocephaline 89, 90, 92, 115, 116, 117
Lesser Ritual of the Pentagram 15, 29, 30, 31
Levi, Eliphas 10, 14, 23, 29, 30, 32, 58

M

Mackey, Albert 5, 6, 13, 19, 36, 48, 49, 50, 60, 64, 84, 90, 98, 99, 109, 110, 111, 112, 113, 116, 117
Macrocosm 4, 10, 11, 29, 42, 48, 69
Magian 4
Magick 3, 4, 7, 8, 9, 10, 11, 13, 14, 15, 16, 17, 20, 21, 22, 23, 25, 27, 29, 31, 34, 36, 37
Magus 16, 24, 27
Mandalas 19
Master Mason 5, 32, 33, 65, 66, 67, 72, 86, 99, 115
Mathers, Samuel Liddell MacGragor 9, 17, 23, 27, 69
Mercury 15, 45, 85, 87, 113, 117
Microcosm 3, 10, 29, 42, 48, 69
Middle Pillar 14
Minoan Civilization 84
Mithraism 4, 28, 34, 35, 36, 45, 46, 89, 90, 109, 111, 112, 113, 114, 115, 116, 118, 119
Mithras 36, 46, 58, 72, 89, 90, 92, 95, 109, 112, 115, 116, 117, 118, 119
Modes of Recognition 17, 53

N

Natural Magic 7, 8, 9
New Thought 4

O

Obligation 17
Odysseus 84
Operative Stonemasonry 5, 6, 20
Orden des Gold und Rosenkreutz 24
Order of the Eastern Star 62
Orders of Architecture 82
Ordo Templi Orientis 9, 17, 21
Orpheus 85, 91, 95
Orphic Mysteries 91, 95
Osiris 69, 70, 71, 84, 90, 93, 95

P

Paracelsus 15
Pentagram 15, 29, 30, 31, 62
Pentagrammaton 62
Persephone 83, 85, 95, 100
Pike, Albert 3, 20, 23, 36, 45, 46, 62, 64, 71, 103, 112, 113, 116
Point Within A Circle 19, 46, 64, 116
Pomegranates 83
Poseidon 79
Prima Materia 15
Psychology 103
Psychopompos 85, 86

Q

Qabalah 21, 23
Quadrivium 42, 65, 111, 113
Qur'an 27, 28

R

Royal Arch 31, 32, 46, 56, 57, 69, 72

S

Saints John 31, 46, 56, 59, 64, 116
Salt, Sulfur and Mercury 15
Sanctum Sanctorum 13, 66, 67, 69, 72
Sephirah 18
Sephiroth 24, 25
Shamash 88
Sigils 19, 27
Sirius 57, 62, 94, 95
Societas Rosicruciana 9, 16, 23, 24, 31, 32, 36, 115
Solar Allegory 29, 95, 118
Sol Invictus 88, 92, 115
Solomon 6, 13, 14, 20, 27, 28, 59, 65, 66, 67, 72, 83, 84, 111
Solstices 30, 31, 46, 47, 49, 50, 56, 58, 59, 61, 69, 93, 118
Supreme Being 18, 28, 29
Sympathetic Magic 79

T

Tabula Smaragdina 10, 47
Tanakh 16

Taurian Age 45, 56, 58, 69, 116
Tauroctony 36, 46, 115, 116
Templar 15
Temple 4, 6, 11, 12, 13, 14, 18, 20, 27, 36, 48, 49, 59, 65, 66, 67, 69, 70, 71, 72,
      83, 84, 98, 110, 111
Temple of Solomon 6
Tetragrammaton 17, 30, 62
Tetramorph 29, 31, 32, 46, 56
Theseus 84, 85
Theurgy 28
Third Degree 65, 99
Thoth 12, 87, 88, 91
Tragedy 20, 97
Tree of Life 14, 23
Trestleboard 66

U

Underworld 29, 83, 85, 87, 95, 97, 100

V

Venus 45, 62, 63, 94, 113
Vitruvius 82
Volume of Sacred Law 16, 63

W

Westcott, William Wynn 9, 23
Woodman, William Robert 9
Working Tools 7, 65, 90, 111, 113

Z

Zeus 79, 88, 91, 99
Zoroastrianism 45, 111, 115

ABOUT THE AUTHOR

Jaime Paul Lamb was raised in St Johns Lodge no. 6, F.&A.M., Norwalk, CT. He currently resides in Phoenix, AZ and is a member of Ascension Lodge UD, Arizona Lodge no. 2, Phoenix York Rite bodies, AZ College of S.R.I.C.F., Arizona Research Lodge no. 1 and Lapis Lazuli Oasis, O.T.O..

CONTACT

To inquire about speaking engagements, lecture presentations, podcast/ radio appearances, article solicitations or other opportunities, please email the author directly at: jaimepaullamb@hotmail.com.